# Saving Pan

## By The Grant Park Chapter of Roots & Shoots

Making the world a better place for chimps
(and the rest of us), one vegetarian recipe at a time

## Dedication

For the orphaned chimpanzees, that they may have the care they need to recover and thrive.

# Table of Contents

03 Dedication

07 Foreward

09 Introduction

97 Acknowledgments

## Chapter 1: Breakfast

**15 Quelites Greens with Egg, Salsa Verde, & Corn Tortillas**
*Kelly Myers, Xico, Portland, OR*

**16 Monkey Bread**
*Matisse Nash*

**17 Buckenmeyer Family Yeasted Waffles**
*Lily Buckenmeyer*

**19 Berry Smoothie**
*Jonathan Grumbles, Laughing Planet Cafe, Portland, OR*

**20 Hot-Cold Eggs with Maple Syrup**
*Alain Passard, L'Arpège, Paris, France*

**21 Swedish Pancakes**
*Ruby Cooper-Karl*

**23 Pumpkin Spice Pancakes**
*Kim Boyce, Bake Shop, Author of "Good to the Grain," Portland, OR*

**24 Puffed Apple Pancakes**
*Martha Bulkeley*

**25 Becky's Quiche**
*McKenzie Caldicott*

**27 Any Veggie Frittata**
*Michael Pollan, "The Omnivore's Dilemma"*

**28 Lemon-Raspberry Poppyseed Bread**
*John Blomgren and Garrett Jones, Back to Eden Bakery, Portland, OR*

## Chapter 2: Small Bites

**31 Watermelon Gazpacho**
*Daphne Cheng, Suite ThreeOhSix, NYC*

**32 Panisse**
*Thomas Keller, French Laundry, Yountville, CA*

**33 I Am Happy Almond Hummus**
*Terces and Matthew Engelhart, Café Gratitude, Berkeley, CA*

**34 Savory Vegetable Milhojas**
*Luis Laplaza Hernandez-Franch and Ángel Custodio Ruiz Seville, Spain*

**35 Chilled Tofu with Scallions, Cantaloupe, & Hot Bean Paste**
*Sarah Pliner, Aviary, Portland, OR*

## Chapter 3: Salads, Soups And Sides

**39 Apple & Fennel Salad**
*Alex Yoder, Olympia Provisions, Portland, OR*

**40 Oliver's Cucumber Salad**
*Jason Stoller Smith, Timberline Lodge, Mt. Hood, OR*

**41 Roasted Brussels Sprouts**
*Maya Rashid*

**43 Lacinato Kale Salad**
*Jenn Louis, Ray, Portland, OR*

**44 Cauliflower in Lemon Coconut Fennel Sauce**
*Roy Farmer, The Green Door Restaurant, Ottawa, Ontario*

**45 Chickpea Salad**
*Nick Davis, The Wild Cow, Nashville, TN*

**47 White House Kitchen Garden Cucumber Soup**
*Michelle Obama, White House Kitchen, Washington, DC*

48 **Lentil Minestrone with Kale**
*Martha Rose Shulman, NY Times Recipes for Health*

49 **Potato Quinoa Soup**
*Charlotte Stoeger*

51 **Moroccan Chickpea Soup**
*Annie Somerville, Greens, San Francisco, CA*

53 **Kasha Pilaf**
*Kevin Archer, Catskill Animal Sanctuary Compassionate Cuisine Program, Saugerties, NY*

55 **Roasted Parsnips and Carrots**
*Ina Garten, "Barefoot Contessa Back to Basics"*

## Chapter 4: Main Dishes

59 **Soba Sensation**
*Leslie McEachern, Angelica Kitchen, NYC*

60 **Mushroom Popover Pie**
*Mollie Katzen, "The Heart of the Plate"*

61 **Talia's Mix & Match Pesto Pasta**
*Talia Baskin*

63 **Lime Tofu Wraps**
*George Schaller, Primatologist, Museum of Natural History, NYC*

65 **Aunt Debbie's Artichoke Lasagna**
*Maeve Larco*

67 **Vegetarian Angel Hair Pasta**
*Jane Goodall, The Jane Goodall Institute*

68 **Idaho Chili**
*Maren Jackson, Seva Restaurant, Ann Arbor, MI*

69 **Grandpa Eastman's Macaroni & Cheese**
*McKenzie Tell*

71 **Quinoa and Chickpea Burgers**
*Jaco Smith, Lechon, Portland, OR*

73 **Creamy Mac 'N Cheeze**
*Heidi Lovig, Heidi Ho Organics, Portland, OR*

74 **Sweet Potato Curry**
*Becky Atkins, Stella Taco, Portland, OR*

77 **Chili Verde**
*Eric Bell, Standing Stone Brewing Co., Ashland, OR*

78 **Skillet Spanakopita**
*Mark Bittman, "How to Cook Everything Fast"*

79 **Spinach Stuffed Portobello Bowls**
*Danielle Primo, Minirette, Seattle, WA*

80 **Alboronia (Ratatouille)**
*Ángel Custodio Ruiz, Enrique Becerra, Seville, Spain*

## Chapter 5: Desserts

83 **French Apple Cake**
*Papa Haydn's, Portland, OR*

84 **Carrot Cake with Cream Cheese Frosting**
*Willa Gagnon*

85 **Mini Key Lime Pie**
*Brooke Abbruzzese*

87 **Peanut Butter Cookies**
*Karen Pride, Harlow Restaurant, Portland, OR*

88 **Rambo's Rice Crispy Treats**
*Linda Soper Kolton, Catskill Animal Sanctuary Compassionate Cuisine Program, Saugerties, NY*

90 **Raw Chocolate Almond Joy**
*Jia Patton, "Celebrate Life!"*

91 **Snickerdoodles**
*Hanna Stokes*

93 **Skillet Blackberry-Blueberry Cobbler**
*Emma Francioch*

95 **Chocolate Bliss Macaroons**
*Jia Patton, "Celebrate Life!"*

**Foreword**

# The Importance of Plant-Based Eating

**"**

We need to think more about the food we eat. I became a vegetarian because of the horrible cruelty to animals on the factory farms. But as well, forests are destroyed for grazing, or to grow the grain to feed the several billion animals raised for meat. It is very wasteful of water and fossil fuels. And the animals produce methane, a powerful greenhouse gas. As a species, we are eating too much and too cheap of meat at this time. If we eat less or none we are truly helping the planet, and we shall be healthier, too.

**"**

— **Jane Goodall** *Ph.D., DBE*
*Primatologist, Ethologist, Anthropologist, and UN Messenger of Peace.*
*Founder of the Jane Goodall Institute and the world's foremost expert on chimpanzees.*

# Introduction

**Bushmeat** /ˈbʊʃˌmiːt/ *Noun*
*Meat taken from any animal native to African forests, including species that may be endangered or not usually eaten outside Africa.*

If the term "bushmeat" is new to you, you're not alone. One of our goals for this cookbook is to educate people about the detrimental effects of the bushmeat trade and bring the "Bushmeat Crisis" to the eyes of the public.

In Africa, the forest is often referred to as "the bush," and bushmeat is the term for meat from the wild animals in the forest. But commercial hunting of these wild animals, many of which are endangered, is illegal. Unfortunately, this doesn't stop bushmeat traders, and commercial hunting is becoming one of the main threats to wildlife in Africa.

In the Congo and Democratic Republic of the Congo, the bushmeat trade has a very large impact on primates like chimpanzees, leading to a loss of wildlife, the spread of disease, and the expansion of bushmeat hunting in other countries.

When mother chimps are killed for their meat, their babies are left to fend for themselves. But these young chimps strongly depend on their mothers when they are young, and usually cannot survive alone. With adult chimpanzees hunted for their meat, and their babies unable to survive without them, the population of this endangered species is declining way too fast.

The hunting of bushmeat not only affects chimpanzees, it also affects those who consume their meat. For example, one big problem for the consumers of bushmeat is the spread of disease. Research shows that wild chimps in Cameroon are naturally infected with Simian Foamy Virus, a virus that people think may have spread HIV to humans. Many think through this contact with primate blood, and consuming bushmeat, this disease was transmitted to people. Animals used as bushmeat have also been known to spread other diseases such as smallpox, chicken pox, tuberculosis, and measles. Scientists speculate that all of these diseases are spread through contact with blood and other liquids from undercooked bushmeat.

If the bushmeat trade is harmful to the environment and to humans, why does it still exist? Many poor citizens cannot afford, or have access to, sustainable protein sources, and are dependent on bushmeat for food. Also, some people hunt these wild animals to make a living. They sell it to those who need the food because they need the money. However, most people doing this are unaware that it is illegal and harmful to the environment. There have been many cases where hunters who used to hunt chimps vowed to stop hunting them after being informed about the consequences to the environment and how harmful it is to baby chimps.

We understand that lots of people don't have any choice other than to kill or sell chimps for food and money. That being said, we can still make an impact by raising awareness at the government level, so that the leaders in charge can find ways to help the people find the food and wages they need, without resorting to bushmeat. For example, people need to be educated about how to hunt non-endangered animals, and do so in a way that does not eliminate the species, so that chimps and other endangered animals can thrive.

## How This Cookbook Can Help

As teens living in the United States, we can't directly educate the people who are involved in the bushmeat trade, or supply the country with a more sustainable protein choice. But we can help in other ways, and that's where this cookbook comes in.

Saving Pan is a vegetarian cookbook we have created to raise money and awareness for the orphaned chimps in Africa. All of the profits will go to Jane Goodall's Tchimpounga Sanctuary to help transport orphaned baby chimps to the sanctuary to receive the help they need.

Tchimpounga is a safe haven for chimps in Pointe Noire, Republic of the Congo. The sanctuary was created by the Jane Goodall Institute in order to care for and provide a home for orphaned chimps rescued from the black market. The sanctuary started in 1992, and The Jane Goodall Institute had to have the government of the Republic of the Congo's consent on this project. It is the largest sanctuary on the African continent. It was originally designed to hold 30 chimps but now it holds around 150 orphaned chimps and eight adult chimps. By donating money to this cause through the sales of our cookbook, we hope to help care for some of the chimps. And by highlighting the issues related to the bushmeat crisis, we hope to educate the public and create a ripple effect of change around the world.

### How Saving Pan Was Born

We were looking for a way to help spread the word about the bushmeat crisis as well as raise funds to help orphaned chimpanzees. Creating a cookbook that required no meat at all, and selling copies of it to raise money for chimps, seemed like a good first step. Plus, creating a cookbook sounded like fun!

This cookbook, filled with delicious vegetarian recipes from top chefs as well as our own family kitchens, was three years in the making. We started working on it in 6th grade and finished at the end of 8th grade. We learned many life skills in the process. We started by writing to chefs, food activists and primatologists and asked if they would contribute a vegetarian recipe to our cookbook. Then we spent hours cooking in the kitchen on Friday nights, testing the recipes and eating together. In our final year we worked on planning and writing the book, from the introduction to the headnotes. Then we worked with a photographer on food styling and food photography. Through it all we learned the importance of teamwork, cooperation, research and advocacy. Plus we were introduced to ingredients and dishes we had never tasted before.

You might be wondering, why did we name the book Saving Pan? It turns out, "pan" has several different meanings that all relate to our project:

- A broad, shallow, and open container for cooking
- The genus name for the two species of apes known as chimpanzees
- A character in a popular children's story about lost childhood

The first one, a cooking pan, has an obvious connection to the cookbook. Number two, the genus name for chimps, has an obvious connection to the chimps we're hoping to help. But the connection to the third definition, a reference to Peter Pan, might not be so clear. Well, think of it this way: Peter Pan was an orphaned child, similar to the orphaned chimps in Africa. It's our biggest hope that they can go on to thrive as well as he did.

**-The Grant Park Chapter of Roots & Shoots:**

*Brooke, Charlotte, Emma, Hanna, Lily, Maeve, Martha, Matisse, Maya, McKenzie C, McKenzie T, Ruby, Talia, and Willa*

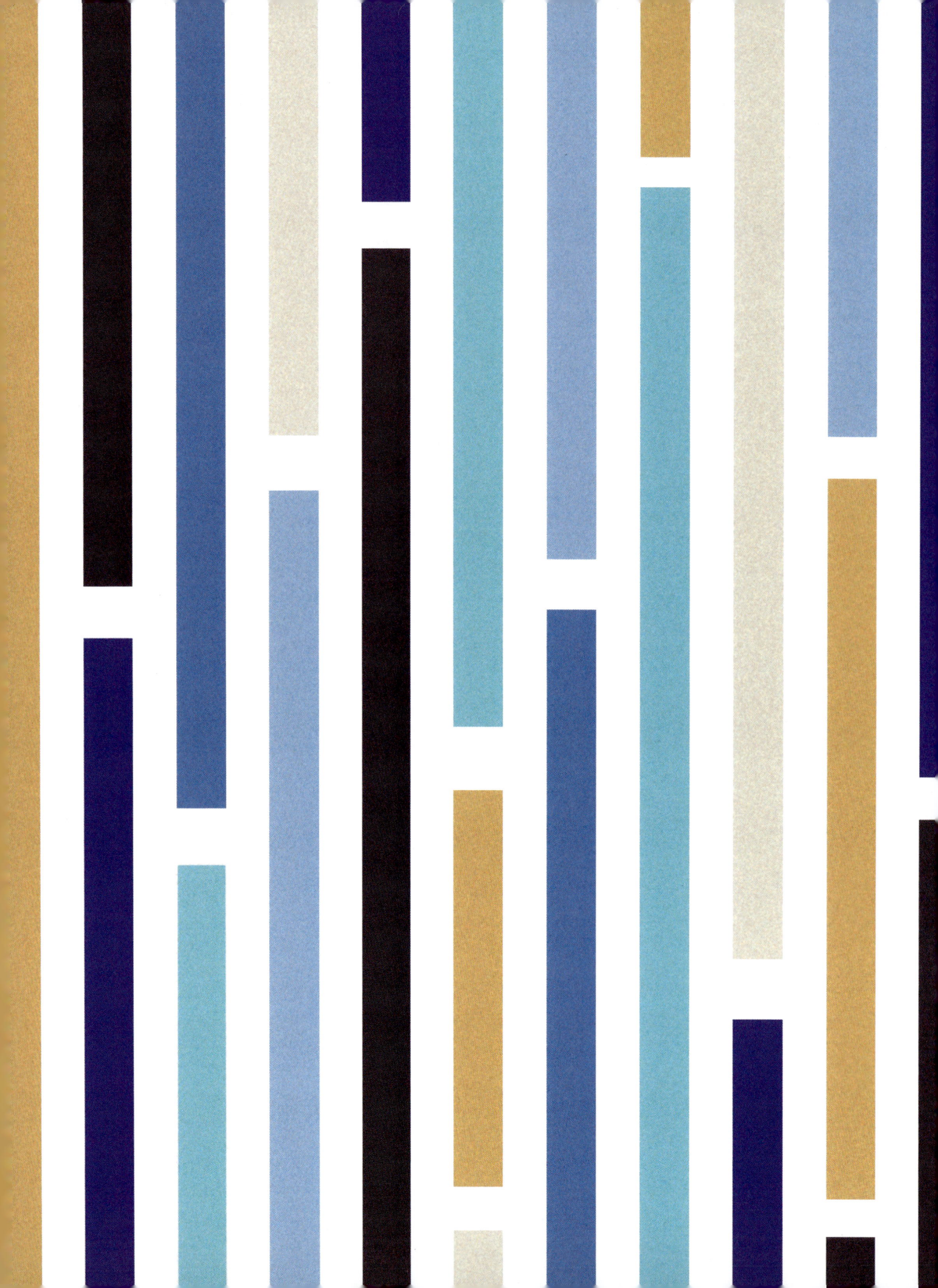

**Chapter 1**

# Breakfast

When it comes to breakfast, it should be something so good it motivates you to get up. And if there's one thing that could get us up and out of bed without complaint it's pancakes, especially the Pumpkin Spice Pancakes shared with us by Portland chef Kim Boyce. But that's just the beginning. From fruity smoothies to veggie-packed fritattas, this chapter has a wide range of dishes to start your day off right.

# Quelites with Egg, Salsa Verde & Corn Tortillas

*Serves 4 to 6 as a light breakfast, appetizer, or side dish.*

**Kelly Myers**
*Xico, Portland, OR*

*Kelly Myers is a chef at Xico, a Mexican restaurant in Portland, Oregon. They take a very hands-on approach to cooking and even grind organic corn flour to make their tortillas. It's standard Mexican food that has been elevated to make it a bit more interesting and flavorful.*

Eggs, spinach, and salsa — what a perfect and power-packed breakfast! The chilies and salsa give these eggs a bit of a kick. If you like a little heat, you won't be disappointed. In Mexico "quelites" refers to amaranth greens, but it's come to be used as a term for any mix of tender sautéed greens.

2 Tbsp extra-virgin olive oil

½ cup finely chopped white onions

1 to 2 serrano or jalapeño chiles, finely chopped

2 bunches rainbow chard, including stems, thinly sliced crosswise into 1/8-inch-wide pieces

¾ tsp kosher salt

2 roma tomatoes, diced

3 eggs, lightly beaten

3 Tbsp chopped fresh cilantro

6 Tbsp crema Mexicana or crema Oaxquena

6 Tbsp salsa verde at room temp. *See recipe on next page, or use store-bought.*

8 to 12 corn tortillas
*Enough for 2 per person*

Heat the oil in a wide pot set over medium-high heat. Add 6 tablespoons of the onion and the chilies. Sauté until edges of onion turn golden. Add sliced greens and salt and mix with the onion and chilies. Sauté until greens wilt but are not soggy. Add the tomato and egg and stir to combine. Cook until the egg is set. Stir in remaining 2 tablespoons onion and the cilantro.

Meanwhile, warm corn tortillas in batches in a skillet over medium heat, turning them once. Remove hot tortillas to a basket or bowl lined with a clean kitchen towel. Fold towel over the tortillas to keep them warm.

Serve greens in a bowl with crema spooned over the top. Set salsa verde (recipe on next page) on the table with the basket of tortillas for guests to serve themselves.

*See Salsa Verde recipe on next page >*

**Salsa Verde** continued...

½ lb tomatillos, husks removed

2 serrano chiles with seeds, chopped

2 Tbsp chopped white onion

1 clove garlic, chopped

1/3 cup roughly chopped fresh cilantro

1 tsp kosher salt

Bring a medium pot of water to a boil over high heat. Salt generously and add the tomatillos. Boil until soft, about 10 minutes. Drain and let cool. Combine tomatillos in a blender with the remaining ingredients and blend to a slightly textured consistency. Thin with water if desired.

# Monkey Bread

*Serves 8*

**Matisse's Favorite Family Recipe**

We've never met a soul who doesn't love the cinnamon-sugar goodness of monkey bread. And it's super easy to make too. Matisse loves how all the buttery sugary syrup oozes between the balls of dough.

2 loaves of Rhodes frozen white bread dough

½ cup (1 stick) butter, melted and cooled

3/4 cup granulated sugar

3/4 cup packed brown sugar

1 ½ Tbsp cinnamon

Grease two 9-by-5-inch loaf pans. Place a frozen loaf in each one, cover with plastic wrap and allow to thaw overnight at room temperature.

The next morning, preheat oven to 350 degrees F. Cut the thawed and risen dough into bite-size chunks.

In a small mixing bowl, combine both sugars and the cinnamon. Dunk the dough pieces into the melted butter, roll in the sugar mixture, and place in the loaf pans. Stack and layer the dough pieces until they reach 3/4 to the top of the pan. (You can also use a Bundt pan.)

Bake for 20 to 25 minutes, until the top springs back and the dough is cooked through. Wait a few minutes before inverting onto serving plates. Allow guests to serve themselves by pulling off pieces from the loaf.

# Buckenmeyer Family Yeasted Waffles

*Serves 4*

### Lily's Family Favorite
*Adapted slightly from "The Breakfast Book" by Marion Cunningham*

"We love this recipe for sleepovers, special occasions, and large group gatherings because you can do most of the prep the night before," says Lily. "The waffles are crunchy on the outside and light and airy in the middle. And the yeasty smell in the house is both comforting and celebratory." This recipe works best in a standard waffle maker (not Belgian) and can easily be doubled or tripled. If there are any leftover waffles, they freeze well.

½ cup warm water

1 package (2 ¼ tsp) active dry yeast

2 cups whole milk, warmed

1 stick (½ cup) unsalted butter, melted and cooled slightly

1 tsp table salt

1 tsp granulated sugar

2 cups all-purpose flour

2 large eggs, lightly beaten

A dash of vanilla

¼ tsp baking soda

Pour the water into a large mixing bowl (the batter will rise to double its volume so you need a large bowl). Sprinkle the yeast over the water, and let stand to dissolve for 5 minutes.

Add the milk, butter, salt, sugar, and flour, and whisk until well blended and smooth. Cover the bowl with plastic wrap, and let it stand overnight at room temperature.

When you're ready to eat, preheat a waffle maker. (We usually cook them on the hottest setting.) Add the eggs, vanilla, and baking soda, and stir to mix well. The batter will be very thin (so runny you may worry that you did something wrong. Not to worry!). Pour an appropriate amount of batter into your hot waffle maker (this amount will vary from machine to machine). Cook until golden brown.

# Berry Smoothie

*Serves 2*

**Jonathan Grumbles**
*Laughing Planet Cafe, Portland, OR*

*Jonathan Grumbles is a chef at Laughing Planet, a restaurant with locations in Oregon and a few locations in Nevada. Their food is simple and family-friendly—and also very nutritious and delicious. Their goal is to have all of their food be organic, fresh, and local. They are very flexible about adjusting their meals to fit all different dietary restrictions*

This smoothie is perfect in summer, but also is enjoyable on a cool autumn day. The fresh ginger adds a touch of spice to the sweet berries. Packed with vitamins and antioxidants, it's the perfect thing to fuel you up for the day ahead.

10 oz apple juice
Or other juice of your choice.

2 oz fresh or frozen strawberries

2 oz fresh or frozen blueberries

2 oz fresh or frozen blackberries

1 oz fresh or frozen banana

1 Tbsp fresh grated ginger, optional

Blend all ingredients together until very smooth. Divide among glasses and serve.

# Hot-Cold Eggs with Maple Syrup

*Serves 8*

**Alain Passard**
*L'Arpège, Paris, France*

*Alain Passard is a French chef and owner of L'Arpège restaurant in Paris. His focus on color, shape, odor and taste elevate his cooking to an art. His move to introduce menus with vegetables at the center of the plate was revolutionary in fine dining establishments, and his desire to work with quality ingredients led him to develop gardens for his restaurant produce. His restaurant self-manages its vegetable, herb, and fruit production and produces more than 40 tons of produce annually.*

This fancy, rich and unusual French dish offers an interesting combination of temperatures and flavors. It's even served in an egg shell! The warm egg yolks are topped with cold whipped cream, and the dish is seasoned with a savory-sweet mix of fresh chives, baking spices and maple syrup. Although most of us found it delicious, it is an acquired taste and may not be for everyone.

8 large eggs

1 cup heavy cream

Small pinch flaky sea salt

Pinch of ground ginger

Pinch of ground white pepper

Pinch of nutmeg

Pinch of cloves

1 Tbsp sherry vinegar

1 Tbsp chopped fresh chives

Maple syrup, for drizzling

With an egg topper (an eggshell punch tool), delicately score 8 eggs, leaving a clean line around each shell. Then, with the corner of a razor blade, go a little deeper, following the demarcated line to take the top of the shell off. Carefully pour the egg whites into a clean, dry bowl, using your fingers like a strainer over the opening of the shell to keep the yolk from coming out. Place the eggshells in an egg carton, cover with plastic wrap, and refrigerate until ready to cook. (You will not use the whites in this recipe, so refrigerate or freeze them for another use.)

In chilled medium metal bowl, combine 1 cup of heavy cream with the fleur de sel, ginger, pepper, nutmeg, cloves, and vinegar. With a whisk or a hand-mixer fitted with a whisk attachment, whip the cream until just thickened enough to coat the back of a spoon. Taste and adjust the spices and vinegar to your taste. Transfer to a pastry bag fitted with a plain tip, or a ziptop bag that you can cut the corner from, and refrigerate until ready to serve.

Fill a large saucepan halfway with water and warm over low heat to 160 degrees F. Place the eggshells in the steaming water. (They will float like tiny ships!) Cook for 3 to 4 minutes, until the yolks are warm and thickened, but still runny like a soft-boiled egg. (Watch the edges of the yolks; a white line will form.)

Carefully remove from the water and place each shell in an egg cup. Sprinkle with chopped chives. Pipe a generous dollop of the spiced whipped cream on top. Drizzle lightly with maple syrup. Serve immediately.

To eat, insert a small demitasse spoon all the way into the shell to get a bit with the warmth of the egg yolk and the chill of the cream.

# Swedish Pancakes

*Serves 4*

### Ruby's Family Favorite

These pancakes have a delightful, chewy texture and are so good with both savory and sweet fillings. Ruby's family likes to cook these for a delicious start to the weekend.

3 eggs

1 Tbsp vegetable oil

1 cup milk

2/3 cup all-purpose flour

Dash of salt

4 Tbsp unsalted butter

Preheat oven to 200° F. In a medium mixing bowl, beat the eggs, oil, and milk until well combined. Whisk in the flour and salt until smooth.

Set a 10-inch sauté pan over medium-low heat. Add a teaspoon of butter and turn the pan to coat. Add 1/2 cup of batter and swirl the pan to coat the bottom. Cook until the pancake sets and the edges are crisp, about 2 minutes. Use a rubber spatula to carefully lift the pancake and flip it over. Cook until the other side is golden, about 1 minute more. Transfer to a plate and keep warm in the oven. Repeat with the remaining butter and batter, stacking the pancakes on the plate in the oven as you go.

Fold each pancake into fourths and serve with jam, fresh fruit, lemon curd, or syrup.

# Pumpkin Spice Pancakes

Serves 4

**Kim Boyce**
Bake Shop, Portland, OR
From the cookbook "Good to the Grain"

*Kim Boyce is the owner of Bakeshop in Portland, OR, and won a James Beard Award for her cookbook "Good to the Grain". Her whole grain philosophy has revolutionized pastry baking and offers unexpected flavors and textures in every bite.*

These pancakes are a good twist on traditional pancakes. The pumpkin is beautifully mixed in with warm, seasonal spices to create a delicious combination of flavors. A sprinkling of spiced sugar on top, and a nice drizzle of maple syrup make these pancakes a great fall breakfast.

1 cup kamut flour
or white whole wheat flour

1 cup all-purpose flour
or white whole wheat flour

2 tsp baking powder

1 tsp kosher salt

1/2 tsp baking soda

1/2 tsp cinnamon

1/8 tsp allspice

1 1/4 cup whole milk

1 cup buttermilk

2/3 cup pumpkin puree

2 Tbsp honey

2 eggs

3 Tbsp unsalted butter, melted, plus more for cooking

Chocolate chips, optional

In a large bowl, whisk all the dry ingredients together until well combined.

In a medium bowl, mix all the wet ingredients except the butter together until well combined.

Gently fold the wet into the dry using a light and gentle touch (for tender and fluffy pancakes). Stir in the melted butter.

In a small bowl, mix all the spiced sugar ingredients together until well combined. (Recipe on next page.)

Heat a griddle or large sauté pan over medium heat for several minutes until hot (sprinkle a few drops of water on the pan and they should bounces a few times before sizzling away.) Lightly brush with butter. Use a ladle or 1/4 cup measuring cup to spoon the batter onto the griddle. Cook until bubbles begin to pop and the edges look a little dry, then flip over and cook the other side until pancakes are cooked through, about 1 minute more. (You can keep the pancakes warm in a 200 degree F oven until ready to serve.)

*See Spiced Sugar recipe on next page >*

**Spiced Sugar** continued...

1/3 cup granulated sugar

2 tsp freshly grated nutmeg

3/4 tsp cinnamon

1/4 tsp allspice

To serve with pancakes, sprinkle a small amount of the spiced sugar on top of the pancakes and pass the extra at the table.

# Puffed Apple Pancakes

*Serves 4-6*

**Martha's Family Favorite**

"The pancake looks very puffy and huge in the oven," says Martha, "and when you take it out it stays puffed for a few seconds before it begins to deflate. Don't miss that part! It's awesome! This is one of my favorite things to eat."

2 tart apples
*Such as Granny Smith.*

¾ cup pastry flour

½ tsp ground cinnamon

2 Tbsp granulated sugar

¼ tsp kosher salt

4 large eggs

1 cup milk

1 tsp vanilla extract

2 Tbsp unsalted butter, melted and cooled

4 Tbsp cold unsalted butter

Powdered sugar, for garnish

Preheat oven to 425 degrees F. Peel, core and slice the apples into 16 pieces.

In a medium bowl, combine flour, cinnamon, sugar and salt. In a separate bowl, whisk together the eggs, milk, vanilla and melted butter. Add the dry mixture and whisk smooth.

Heat 3 tablespoons of the cold butter in a sauté pan. Add the apple slices and sauté for 5 minutes, until tender and golden. Add the remaining tablespoon of butter. When the butter is foaming, pour the batter into the pan and immediately place it in the preheated oven.

Bake the pancake for 15 to 20 minutes, until puffed and golden brown. Sift some powdered sugar on top and serve the pan on a trivet on the table.

*Pear-Almond Variation:* Use pears instead of apples and 1 teaspoon almond extract instead of the vanilla. Sprinkle the pancake with 2 tablespoons of sliced almonds before putting it into the oven.

# Becky's Quiche

*Serves 6*

## McKenzie C's Family Favorite

Perfect for brunch, this cheese and spinach filled tart is a favorite of McKenzie's family. The crust is adapted from Martha Stewart and the filling is adapted from Smitten Kitchen.

*Crust*

2 1/2 cups all-purpose flour

1 tsp salt

1 cup (2 sticks) cold unsalted butter, cut into small pieces

1/4 cup cold water, plus more if needed

*Filling*

3 oz cream cheese, room temperature

1/2 cup heavy whipping cream

4 eggs

10 oz frozen chopped spinach, thawed, excess moisture squeezed out

3/4 cup grated cheese
*Such as a mix of mozzarella, Gruyère and Parmesan.*

1 leek thinly sliced or 4 to 6 scallions

1/4 tsp salt

*To make the crust:* Using a food processor, combine flour and salt. Add the butter pieces, coating each in flour mixture. Pulse until the mixture resembles coarse sand or crumbs. With the machine running, add ice water until the dough is crumbly and just holds together.

Divide the dough into six pieces, flatten them into thick discs, and wrap in plastic wrap (or flatten the dough into 1 disc if making a large tart). Refrigerate for 1 hour.

*To make the filling:* In a medium bowl, beat the cream cheese with a hand-held mixer until smooth. Gradually beat in the heavy whipping cream and eggs. Mix in remaining ingredients.

*To assemble:* Preheat oven to 425 degrees F.

On a lightly floured surface, roll out the dough disc(s) into a circle about ¼-inch thick. (You may need to flip the dough over and re-flour the surface a few times.)

Transfer to tart six 4-inch or one 9-inch tart pan with a removable bottom(s). Lightly press into the bottom and up the sides. Roll the rolling pin across the top of the tart pan(s) to cut off the excess dough and make it flush with the top of the pan. Use a fork to prick a few holes in the bottom.

Pour filling mixture into prepared crusts. Bake until crusts are golden brown and filling is set, about 30 minutes. Cool slightly before popping out of the tart pans and serving.

# Any Veggie Frittata

*Serves 4-6*

**Michael Pollan**
*Author of "The Omnivore's Dilemma"*

*Michael Pollan is an accomplished author, journalist, and professor. Some of his books include: The Omnivore's Dilemma, In The Defense Of Food: An Eater's Manifesto, and Food Rules: An Eater's Manual. He also writes articles about the food industry and agriculture for the New York Times magazine. He has received the Genesis Award, from the Humane Society of the United States, the Reuters World Conservation Union Global Awards in environmental journalism, and the James Beard Foundation Awards for best magazine series. He has also been interviewed for documentaries, and co-starred in Food Inc.*

Perfect for a chilly day, this delectable frittata is a favorite of ours. It has a wonderful texture and is easy to make. It's as great for breakfast as it is for dinner. And the leftovers make for a great lunch. This is a great way to get your vegetables in a delicious package.

1 Tbsp extra-virgin olive oil or butter

1 small onion, diced, or 1 leek, sliced

3 cups chopped vegetables
*Such as spinach, kale, asparagus, summer squash, peppers, par-boiled potatoes, mushrooms, & frozen vegetables are also fine.*

Salt and pepper to taste

8 eggs

Splash of milk

1/4 cup chopped fresh herbs
*Such as chives, Italian (flat-leaf) parsley, tarragon, or basil.*

1 cup grated cheese, optional

Salad and crusty bread, for serving

Preheat oven to 400 degrees F. Set a large sauté pan or cast iron pan over medium-high heat. Add the oil or butter, and the onions or leeks. Sauté until soft, about 10 minutes. Add the vegetables to the pan and sauté a few minutes more, until tender. Season with salt and pepper to taste.

In a medium mixing bowl, whisk the eggs, milk and herbs together until well combined. Season with salt and pepper. Pour the egg mixture over the vegetables and sprinkle with cheese, if using. Let cook for a two or three minutes to let a crust form, then transfer to the oven for ten minutes, or until set.

You can flip the pan over to release the whole frittata onto a serving plate, or cut slices from the pan like a pie. Serve with salad and crusty bread.

# Lemon Raspberry Poppyseed Bread

*Makes 1 loaf or 8 muffins*

**John Blomgren and Garrett Jones**
*Back to Eden Bakery, Portland, OR*

*Back to Eden Bakery and Café in Portland, OR was founded by John Blomgren and Garrett Jones with the goal of providing food that everyone can eat, while planting something in return. They created a thriving model of small scale urban farming and a cottage industry that provides delicious food free of gluten, wheat, dairy, eggs, meat and other common allergens. They proudly serve the greatest number of people they can with their universally delicious food.*

3½ cups all-purpose gluten-free flour

2 Tbsp poppyseeds

1 Tbsp plus 1 tsp baking powder

1 tsp baking soda

½ tsp salt

1¼ cups maple syrup

2/3 cup vegetable oil

½ cup applesauce

½ cup alternative milk
*Such as soy or almond milk.*

Zest of 2 lemons

¼ cup fresh lemon juice

1 Tbsp lemon extract

1 cup raspberries, fresh or frozen

Preheat oven to 350 degrees F. Grease a 9-by-5-inch loaf pan or a large Bundt pan. Sprinkle with flour to coat and tap out the excess.

In a large bowl, mix together the flour, poppyseeds, baking powder, baking soda and salt. Make a well in the center and add the maple syrup, oil, applesauce, milk, lemon zest, lemon juice and lemon extract. Stir the wet ingredients into the dry, until only small lumps remain. Fold in the raspberries.

Pour the batter into the prepared loaf pan or bundt pan. Bake for 45 to 50 minutes or until a knife inserted in the center comes out clean.

## Chapter 2
# Small Bites

Who doesn't like appetizers? You can mix and match these dishes, along with the various side dishes and main courses in this book, to create amazing combinations. These delicious recipes could go with pretty much anything. In this chapter look for Watermelon Gazpacho, which is a great starter on a hot day, as is the flavor-packed Silken Tofu. One of our all-time favorites is the I Am Happy Almond Hummus, which is great with the crispy Panisse fritters.

Although this chapter is a short one, each dish is worth trying.

# Watermelon Gazpacho

*Serves 8 as an appetizer*

**Daphne Cheng**
*Suite ThreeOhSix, NYC*

*Daphne Cheng focuses her culinary spotlight on fresh, seasonal vegetables and believes that vegetables should be the centerpiece of a meal. Her global flavors are unusual, provoking, and delicious. She founded the Suite ThreeOhSix supper club to offer multi-course dinners based on the freshest vegetables at the moment. This gazpacho sums up her fresh, unique take on food.*

Crisp, juicy watermelon and bright cucumber give this soup a freshness that is perfect for a hot summer day. Served in small cups, it's a lively and refreshing way to kick off a summer meal. To finish this dish, add a pinch of mint on top.

1 (3-lb) seedless watermelon

2 cucumbers

½ cup packed fresh basil, plus more for garnish

2 scallions, ends trimmed, plus more for garnish

1 Tbsp extra-virgin olive oil

Lime juice, to taste

Salt and freshly ground black pepper to taste

Slice off the top and bottom of the melon and place on one end. Cut away the rind around the melon. Cut the flesh into chunks.

Peel the cucumbers, slice in half lengthwise and scoop out the seeds. Cut the flesh of one cucumber into large chunks. Cut the other into small dice and reserve for garnish.

Place the watermelon, cucumber chunks, basil and scallions in a blender and blend until smooth. Drizzle in the olive oil while blending. Add lime juice, salt and pepper to taste.

Cover gazpacho and refrigerate until cold, at least 1 hour and up to 4 hours. To serve, divide among bowls and garnish with the diced cucumber, chopped basil and sliced scallions.

# Panisse

*Serves about 6*

**Thomas Keller**
*The French Laundry, Yountville, CA*

*Thomas Keller is a renowned chef who has received numerous culinary awards, including The Culinary Institute "Chef of the Year", the James Beard Foundation's "Outstanding Chef" and "Outstanding Resturanteur", and Time Magazine's "America's Best Chef". He owns multiple restaurants across the country and has authored five best-selling cookbooks.*

These crispy golden chickpea fritters are addictive. They're crunchy on the outside and soft and moist on the inside. Serve them as an appetizer or snack with something to dip them in, such as sweet pepper puree, herbed yogurt, olive tapenade, tomato sauce, or the almond hummus.

4 cups vegetable broth or water

1 medium clove of garlic

1 Tbsp plus 1 tsp extra-virgin olive oil (plus a little extra to oil the pan)

8 oz (about 2 ½ cups) chickpea flour

1 ½ tsp kosher salt (plus extra for final seasoning

Canola oil for frying

Lightly oil the inside of a 10-inch-square baking dish (or any other similar-sized dish). Place the vegetable broth, garlic, olive oil and salt in the jar of a blender and blend at high speed until the garlic is no longer visible. Continue to blend on medium speed and gradually add the chickpea flour, a little at a time, until it is all incorporated and you reach a smooth batter consistency. (You may have to do this in two batches depending on the size of your blender.)

Pour the batter into a saucepan with tall sides and about 8- to 10-inches in diameter. Set over medium heat and cook, whisking continuously, until the batter thickens. Continue stirring vigorously with the rubber spatula until the batter begins to boil and becomes very thick. Take caution as the batter may splatter a little bit. Immediately transfer the batter to the baking dish and spread it into an even layer using a rubber spatula.

Transfer the baking dish to the refrigerator and allow it to cool uncovered. (Can be prepared up to this point a day ahead).

When ready to serve, carefully unmold the panisse from the baking dish onto a cutting board. Cut into finger-shaped pieces (kind of like fish sticks) and gently pat dry.

Set a heavy-bottomed pot over medium-high heat and pour in enough canola oil to reach 1½ inches deep. Heat the oil to 360 degrees F. Use a slotted spoon or mesh skimmer to carefully immerse a few pieces of the panisse into the hot oil. Fry the panisse until golden brown and crisp. Remove with a wire skimmer and set on a wire rack or paper towels to allow the excess oil to drain off. Sprinkle with kosher salt. Repeat with the remaining pieces. Serve the Panisse very hot with a dip.

# I am Happy Almond Hummus

*Makes 3 cups*

**Terces & Matthew Engelhart**
*Café Gratitude, Berkeley, CA*
*From the cookbook "I am Grateful: Recipes and Lifestyle of Cafe Gratitude"*

*Terces and Matthew Engelhart co-founded the plant-based Café Gratitude restaurants and Gracias Madre in California. They live on Be Love farm where they practice regenerative agriculture to grow organic food. They have several books, including the "I am Grateful: Recipes and Lifestyle of Café Gratitute" cookbook.*

This delicious, creamy hummus was one of our favorite dishes, and so easy to make. We loved customizing the flavor according to our tastes. It's great served with raw veggies like sliced carrots, zucchini and sweet peppers. It's a great dip for the Panisse fritters. And of course it's excellent in sandwiches.

2 1/2 cups soaked almonds, drained and rinsed

¼ cup + 1 tbsp raw tahini

¾ tsp freshly ground black pepper

1 ½ tsp chopped garlic

1 ¾ tsp cumin

¼ cup + 2 tbsp extra-virgin olive oil

¼ cup plus 3 tbsp fresh lemon juice

¾ tsp salt

¾ cup water

Taste the hummus and add more salt, garlic, lemon juice, cumin or olive oil if desired. Serve drizzled with olive oil and dusted with cumin and/or paprika.

# Savory Vegetable Milhojas

*Serves 6*

**Luis LaPlaza Hernandez-Franch & Ángel Custodio Ruiz**
*Seville, Spain*

*Luis Laplaza Hernandez-Franch* teaches the "History of Food" and "Literature of Food" at the University of Seville. *Ángel Custodio Ruiz works at Enrique Becerra in Seville, Spain, where they use high-quality, local ingredients for authentic Southern Spanish cuisine.*

*Milhojas* is the Spanish name for a "thousand layer" cake, but here it applies to a tapa, or snack, made with layers of thinly sliced vegetables. It's really fun to make and eat, and offers a delicious combination of flavors and textures. Tapas were invented as a snack to go with wine or beer, but these are great anytime (especially in the summer). We suggest grating the mozzarella cheese instead of slicing it and sprinkling it on lightly. As for the herbs, chop them very finely so you don't get woody pieces of rosemary in your dish. When shopping for zucchini and tomatoes try to find ones that are the same size diameter, since you'll be stacking the slices. Serve these with a tasty drink and watch them disappear!

2 zucchini, thinly sliced

Extra-virgin olive oil

Salt and freshly ground black pepper

2 Tbsp chopped fresh herbs, *Such as thyme and rosemary.*

2 tart green apples, peeled, cored and thinly sliced

4 roma tomatoes, thinly sliced

8 oz mozzarella cheese, grated

Preheat oven to 400 degrees F. Line a rimmed baking sheet with parchment paper. Arrange the zucchini slices in an even layer, about 1 inch apart (you won't use them all). Brush with olive oil and sprinkle lightly with salt, pepper and some of the herbs.

Stack a slice of tomato on top of each zucchini slice. Sprinkle with salt, pepper and herbs. Add a slice of apple and sprinkle with cheese. Repeat the layering and seasoning with the remaining zucchini, tomato and apple slices. Sprinkle with grated cheese on top.

Bake for 40 to 45 minutes until tender and cooked through, and cheese has browned.

# Chilled Tofu with Scallions, Cantaloupe, & Hot Bean Paste

*Serves 4*

**Sarah Pliner**
*Aviary, Portland, OR*

*Sarah Pliner is a self-trained cook who has drawn on experience and culinary mentors to expand her knowledge. At her restaurant Aviary, she enjoys creating dishes with unfamiliar ingredients or using unusual techniques that allow her guests to experience a flavorful surprise. She includes a fresh vegetable, herb, or fruit component to balance out every meal.*

This gourmet dish of fresh vegetables and soft tofu is delectable. The texture is an interesting combination of flavorful vegetables, and smooth tofu. The contrast of the vibrant vegetables and the vinaigrette drizzled on top will impress your dinner guests. Although you might not have Chinese black vinegar and hot bean paste on hand, they're readily available at Asian markets and are great in stir-fries.

2 (12-oz) packages silken soft tofu, cut half widthwise

¼ cup low-sodium soy sauce

2 Tbsp chinkiang vinegar
*aka Chinese black vinegar*

2 tsp granulated sugar (divided)

3 Tbsp fermented hot bean paste
*Such as O'Long brand.*

3 Tbsp extra-virgin olive oil (divided)

3 scallions, thinly sliced

½ cup diced cantaloupe

2 Tbsp chopped fresh cilantro leaves

2 Tbsp thinly sliced tiato leaves *(see note)*

2 tsp grated fresh ginger

Salt

¼ cup toasted sesame seeds, crushed

¼ cup chopped roasted peanuts

Zest of 1 lime

*See instructions on next page >*

**Chilled Tofu with Scallions, Cantaloupe, and Hot Bean Paste** *continued...*

Place the tofu in the bottom of 3 shallow bowls.

In a small bowl, mix together the soy sauce, black vinegar, and 1 teaspoon sugar. Pour the mixture over the tofu. In the same bowl, mix together the bean paste, 1 tablespoon olive oil, and the remaining 1 teaspoon sugar. Use a spoon to spread the paste on top of each tofu.

In a medium bowl, mix together the scallions, cantaloupe, cilantro, tiato, ginger, and the remaining 2 tablespoons olive oil and season with salt, to taste. Mound on top of each tofu. Garnish each with sesame seeds, peanuts, and lime zest.

*Note:* Tiato is an Asian herb that looks like shiso but is smaller with a purple hue under the leaves and has a similar and stronger flavor. You can usually find it at Asian markets particularly those that specialize in Vietnamese ingredients. If you can't find it, substitute shiso leaves.

**Chapter 3**

# Salads, Soups & Sides

Sometimes a great side dish or salad can really make a meal memorable. And sometimes a simple soup is all it takes to make a meal. That's where this chapter comes in. Whether you're looking to supplement your main dish or cook up a big pot of soup for dinner, there's a wide range of vegetable-packed recipes to choose from.

# Apple & Fennel Salad

*Serves 4-6 as first course*

**Alex Yoder**
*Olympia Provisions, Portland, OR*

*Alex Yoder, a Portland, Oregon native, has worked in many of Portland's best restaurants, including Café Castagna and Clyde Common. He is now the Executive Chef at both of the restaurants owned by Olympia Provisions. Olympia Provisions is Oregon's first USDA approved salumeria. All of their meat is local and high quality.*

Fennel and apples may not be a combination you're used to, but don't let that deter you from making this recipe. The sweetness of the apple blends perfectly with the refreshing fennel and creates a crunchy, savory dish that will surprise and impress your guests.

2 apples
*such as Fuji or Honeycrisp, halved, cored, and sliced 1/8-inch-thick.*

½ head fennel, thinly sliced crosswise on a mandolin

½ cup frisee or endive leaves

2 scallions, sliced thinly on the bias, including half of the green part

3 oz crumbled buttermilk blue cheese

3 Tbsp plus 1 ½ tsp honey

1 Tbsp red wine vinegar

1 Tbsp champagne vinegar

2 Tbsp extra-virgin olive oil

¼ tsp Maldon sea salt, or other flakey sea salt

Freshly ground black pepper to taste

In a large mixing bowl, combine the apples, fennel, frisee, scallions and blue cheese.

In a separate small bowl, combine the honey and both vinegars. Drizzle ¼ cup of the mixture over the apples and fennel; toss to coat evenly. Divide the salad among six plates, taking care to distribute all the ingredients evenly.

Drizzle the olive oil over the salads, dividing it evenly among them. Sprinkle the sea salt over the salads, dividing it evenly among them as well. Crack fresh black pepper over each salad to suit your own taste.

# Oliver's Cucumber Salad with Carrot Dressing

*Serves 4*

**Jason Stoller Smith**
*Timberline Lodge, Mt. Hood, OR*

*Jason Stoller Smith is a self-taught chef who develops close ties with local farmers, ranchers, and vinters to provide sustainable, farm-to-table cuisine. He currently serves as Executive Chef at Oregon's famous Timberline Lodge and has been invited to present at numerous culinary events, including the James Beard Centennial Dinner and a Congressional Picnic on the lawn of the White House.*

There's an exciting mix of flavors and textures in this easy-to-make salad, from the thin slices of cool cucumbers and spicy radishes, to the crunchy edamame and pistachios. The delicious dressing blends up thick and creamy, with natural sweetness from carrots and a little heat from the ginger. You'll have some leftover, which is a good thing! If you have a mandoline slicer, it makes quick work of slicing the vegetables.

*Salad*

2 large cucumbers, sliced very thin

1/4 cup radishes, sliced very thin

1/4 cup edamame beans

1/4 cup shelled pistachios, toasted

1/4 cup Italian (flat-leaf) parsley, stems removed, coarsely chopped

*Dressing*

1 cup vegetable oil

1/2 cup rice wine vinegar

1/4 cup soy sauce

1 Tbsp granulated sugar

1 1/2 tsp finely grated ginger

2 medium carrots, peeled and roughly chopped

1/2 medium yellow onion, roughly chopped

Kosher salt and freshly ground black pepper, to taste

*To make the dressing:* Combine all of the dressing ingredients in a blender or food processor and process until smooth. Season with salt and pepper to taste.

*To make the salad:* Combine all ingredients in a bowl and toss with enough of the dressing to coat lightly and evenly (refrigerate the rest for another salad). Serve immediately.

# Roasted Brussels Sprouts

*Serves 6*

**Maya's Favorite Family Recipe**

Roasting brussels sprouts brings out their sweet side. The shower of grated Parmesan and a squeeze of lemon adds salty-savory brightness.

1½ lbs brussels sprouts

3 to 4 Tbsp extra-virgin olive oil

2 to 3 cloves garlic, coarsely chopped

½ tsp salt, plus more to taste

Red pepper flakes

Freshly ground black pepper

Grated Parmesan cheese, for serving

Fresh lemon juice, for serving

Preheat oven to 400 degrees F. Trim the stem ends and outer leaves from the brussels sprouts. Cut in half lengthwise.

Heat 3 to 4 Tbsp of olive oil in a 12-inch cast iron skillet over medium-high heat. (We prefer more oil so the dish comes out crispy. Adjust to your taste.)

Add the garlic and salt and sauté until fragrant, about 1 minute. Place the brussels sprouts, cut side down, in the skillet. There should be enough room to fit them in a single layer. Add a dash or two of red pepper flakes to taste, and a few grinds of fresh pepper.

Cook for about 4 or 5 minutes, until the brussels sprouts have begun to brown. Transfer the skillet to the oven and roast until the brussels sprouts are tender when pierced with a fork and crispy, about 10 to 15 minutes. Season with more salt and pepper to taste. Serve topped with freshly grated Parmesan cheese and a few squeezes of lemon juice.

# Lacinato Kale Salad

*Serves 4*

**Jenn Louis**
*Ray Restaurant, Portland, OR*

*Jenn Louis celebrates Israel's diverse cuisine at the Ray Restaurant in Portland, OR. She completed on Bravo's "Top Chef Masters", was selected as one of Food and Wine's "Best New Chefs", and has earned two nominations for the James Beard Award of Best Chef: Northwest. Jenn has published two cookbooks, including "The Book of Greens" in 2017.*

The Lacinato kale mixed with nuts and mandarin oranges creates the perfect combination of flavors. The creamy goat cheese ties the whole salad together. This meal makes a good main dish, but also serves as a side for a warm soup.

*Dressing*

2 Tbsp lemon zest

1/3 cup fresh lemon juice

1/2 cup extra-virgin olive oil

Salt and freshly ground black pepper to taste

*Salad*

½ cup pine nuts

½ bunch lacinato kale leaves, stems removed, leaves sliced into ½-inch-wide strips (about 4 cups)

¼ cup thinly sliced shallots

½ cup chévre (fresh goat cheese)

4 satsuma mandarin oranges, peeled and sliced into thin wheels

Flaky sea salt and freshly ground black pepper

*To make the dressing:* In a small bowl or jar with a lid, whisk or shake the dressing ingredients together until well combined. Season with salt and pepper to taste.

*To make the salad:* Set a medium sauté pan over medium-low heat. Add the pine nuts and toast, stirring frequently, until golden brown (watch carefully; they burn easily). Transfer to a large bowl. Add the sliced kale and shallots, and toss to combine. Toss with just enough of the dressing to coat.

Crumble the chévre onto the salad and toss. Divide salad among plates and arrange the satsuma wheels on top. Sprinkle with a little more salt and pepper, and serve.

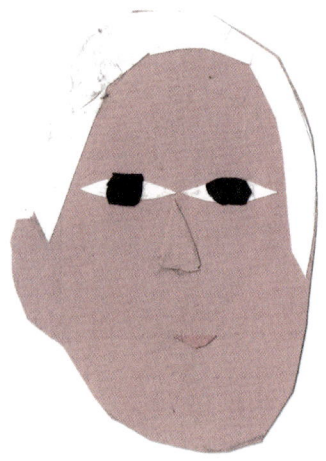

# Cauliflower in Lemon Coconut Fennel Sauce

Serves 4-6

**Roy Farmer**
*The Green Door, Ottawa, Ontario*

*Ron Farmer owns the Green Door Restaurant in Ottawa, Ontario, together with Jenny Ong and Charles Miller. It is a vegetarian restaurant with seasonal harvests on the menu from locally grown organic produce. It was established in 1988 and is Ottawa's oldest Restaurant. Among the three of them they have five decades of experience in the food industry (bakery, restaurant, catering, natural foods store, organic gardening). When describing the philosophy of their restaurant Ron Farmer said, "We specialize in high quality, wholesome foods and baked goods made from ingredients that are locally grown and produced."*

If you're looking for something to warm you up on a rainy autumn day, look no further. This perfectly seasoned roasted cauliflower with a warm, creamy, savory sauce is so delicious, you won't regret trying it.

1 large cauliflower, washed and separated into florets

1/4 cup plus 1 Tbsp extra-virgin olive (divided)

2 tsp salt (divided)

1 medium onion, diced

1 tsp freshly ground fennel seeds

1 (16-oz) can unsweetened coconut milk

Zest of 1 lemon

2 Tbsp fresh lemon juice

Preheat oven to 350 degrees F. In a large bowl, toss the florets with 1 tablespoon of the olive oil and 1 teaspoon of the salt. Arrange in a single layer on a rimmed baking sheet and roast for 20 to 30 minutes, or until wilted and slightly soft.

Heat the remaining ¼ cup olive oil in a large sauté pan over medium heat. Add the diced onions and remaining 1 teaspoon salt. Cook gently for 5 minutes (do not let the onions brown). Add ground fennel and cook a minute longer. Add coconut milk, increase heat to high and bring to a boil. Add roasted cauliflower, lemon zest and lemon juice. Taste and add more lemon juice or salt if desired.

Serve cauliflower sprinkled with a few sprigs of fresh fennel leaves, if available.

# Chickpea Salad

*Serves 6*

**Nick Davis**
*The Wild Cow, Nashville, TN*

*Nick Davis is the head chef at The Wild Cow in Nashville, TN, where he helps to serve vegetarian and vegan food in a casual environment in the heart of the city. The Wild Cow purchases their food in its whole form and makes all of its own sauces, dressing, soup stocks, and more. The Wild Cow aims to bring people together for the love of food in a fun environment, and we couldn't agree more with this mission!*

Freshly cooked or canned and drained chickpeas form a protein-packed base for this creamy, herby salad. It takes just a few minutes to make, and is perfect for school lunches and potlucks.

*Dressing*

1/3 cup Vegenaise (or any vegan mayo)

1/3 cup Dijon mustard

1 Tbsp rice vinegar

1 Tbsp salt

1 tsp freshly ground black pepper

*Salad*

4 cups cooked chickpeas

1/2 red onion, diced

4 stalks celery, diced

1 cup fresh Italian (flat-leaf) parsley, minced

1/4 cup fresh dill, minced

In a large bowl, mash 2 cups of the chickpeas. Stir in the rest of the chickpeas along with the onion, celery, parsley and dill.

In a small mixing bowl, combine the Veganaise, mustard, rice vinegar, salt and pepper. Stir the dressing into the chickpea mixture until well coated. Refrigerate until cold before serving.

# White House Kitchen Garden Cucumber Soup

*Serves 6-8*

**Michelle Obama**
*Washington DC*

*Michelle Obama was the First Lady of the United States from 2008-2016 and is a champion for increasing access to healthy food for all Americans. Her "Let's Move" advocacy campaign aimed to reduce childhood obesity and encourage a healthy lifestyle for children through increased physical activity and access to healthy, affordable food in and out of school. "Let's Move" also worked to improve nutrition labeling and communication so that consumers can make better choices.*

This recipe, which Michelle Obama shared with us while she was First Lady of the United States, is wonderfully cool and creamy. It is has a nice mild flavor, perfect for even the pickiest of eaters.

2 large cucumbers

2 cups almond milk

3 oz plain, whole milk Greek yogurt, plus more for garnish

4 Tbsp chopped fresh dill, plus more for garnish

1/2 tsp salt

Sliced toasted almonds, for garnish

Peel the cucumbers, slice in half lengthwise, scoop out the seeds and coarsely chop. In a blender, combine cucumbers, almond milk, yogurt, dill and salt. Puree until smooth.

Transfer soup to an airtight container and chill until completely cold, at least 1 hour.

To serve, divide the soup among bowls. Garnish with toasted almonds, a dollop of Greek yogurt and a sprig of dill.

# Lentil Minestrone with Kale

*Serves 4-6*

**Martha Rose Shulman**
*"Recipes for Health" columnist for The New York Times*

*Martha Rose Shulman is a cookbook author, cooking teacher, and food columnist who emphasizes fresh, seasonal produce—especially organic options from the farmer's market. She draws culinary inspiration from Mediterranean and Mexican cuisines for their big flavors and adaptability.*

In addition to pasta, this minestrone uses lentils for its starchy component, which means it has even more nutrition and flavor than the old-school classic. If you make it a day ahead, don't add the pasta or rice until you reheat before serving, otherwise it becomes mushy.

- 2 Tbsp extra-virgin olive oil
- 1 small onion, chopped
- 1 large or 2 small carrots, minced (about 3/4 cup)
- Salt to taste
- 4 large garlic cloves, minced
- 1 (14-oz) can tomatoes, seeded and chopped, with juice
- 1/2 tsp dried thyme (or 1 tsp fresh leaves)
- 1/2 tsp oregano
- 1/2 lb lentils (about 1 1/8 cups), picked over and rinsed
- 2 quarts water
- A bouquet garni made with a bay leaf, 1 Parmesan rind, 1/2 tsp dried red pepper, and a couple of sprigs parsley and thyme
- 1/2 lb kale, stalks removed, leaves washed and cut in ribbons (2 cups, tightly packed)
- 1/2 cup small pasta
  *Such as elbow macaroni, small shells or tubetti, or Arborio rice.*
- Freshly ground pepper to taste
- 1/4 cup chopped fresh Italian (flat-leaf) parsley
- Freshly grated Parmesan, for serving

Heat the oil over medium-low heat in a heavy soup pot or Dutch oven, and add the onion and carrot. Cook, stirring, until the vegetables are tender, about 5 minutes or a little longer, and stir in a generous pinch of salt and the garlic. Cook, stirring, just until the garlic smells fragrant and is beginning to color, about 1 minute.

Stir in the tomatoes, thyme, and oregano. Turn the heat to medium and bring the tomatoes to a simmer. Cook, stirring often, for about 10 minutes, until the tomatoes have cooked down somewhat and smell fragrant.

Stir in the lentils and water and bring to a boil.

Add the bouquet garni, reduce the heat, cover and simmer 30 minutes. Add salt, about 2 tsp to begin with (you will probably add more) and the kale, and simmer another 15 minutes, or until the lentils are tender and the broth fragrant.

Stir in the pasta or rice. Continue to simmer another 10 to 15 minutes, until the pasta or rice is cooked through. Grind in some pepper and taste. Is there enough salt? Garlic? Adjust seasonings, and remove the bouquet garni. Stir in the parsley.

Serve, topping each bowlful with a generous spoonful of Parmesan cheese.

# Potato Quinoa Soup

*Serves 6*

### Charlotte's Family Favorite Recipe
*Adapted from "The Art of South American Cooking," by Felipe Rojas-Lombardi*

"This recipe is a favorite for ¾ of our family. We often have it in winter, and its warmth and mild, yet delicious flavor are enjoyed by everyone but my brother. He's crazy, though. Potato Quinoa Soup is good on its own, or as an accompaniment to a salad or protein. Enjoy!"

1 cup uncooked quinoa

2 Tbsp olive oil

2 garlic cloves, minced

1 tsp ground cumin

1 Tbsp coarse sea salt, or 2 tsp regular table salt

1 lb potatoes cut into 1/2" cubes

1/2 lb chopped fresh spinach or chard (optional in our house, but the adults like it)

5 cups water

Juice of 1 orange (optional, but adds depth)

Feta cheese, for serving

Hardboiled eggs, for serving (optional)

Sriracha, for serving (optional)

Thoroughly rinse your quinoa (unless it's pre-rinsed quinoa) and place quinoa plus 2 c water in a pot. Cover with a lid, bring to a boil, then lower heat to a simmer. Cook for 15 minutes.

While your quinoa is cooking, heat your oil on medium heat in a large pot. Add garlic, cumin and salt; cook until fragrant, 1-2 min. Add 5 cups water and bring to a boil. Add potatoes and cook until soft, about 15 minutes.

Once your potatoes are soft, stir in the cooked quinoa, and spinach or chard, if using. Cook for a few minutes, until greens are wilted. Pour in the orange juice and turn off heat.

Serve with crumbled feta on top. If you want it really fancy, add some some slices of hard boiled egg on top when serving, and if you like spice, add some sriracha.

# Moroccan Chickpea Soup

*Serves 8*

**Annie Somerville**
*Greens, San Francisco, CA*

*Annie Somerville is an incredible chef who wrote the books "Field of Greens" and "Everyday Greens"; she is the head chef for the famous vegetarian restaurant, Greens Restaurant. Founded by the Francisco Zen Center in 1979, this restaurant uses delicious, local, organic ingredients. When Greens was founded, most vegetarian places would serve unappetizing salads or other dishes with meat substitutes like tofu. Greens was different--they use vegetables as vegetables, not as meat substitutes. Annie Somerville has also been nominated for both the James Beard Award for Vegetables, Fruits, and Grains, and the James Beard Award for Vegetable Focused and Vegetarian.*

This soup has a warm, spicy flavor, perfect for an autumn evening. Almost everyone who tried this recipe agreed that it was not to be missed. Make this soup for a weeknight dinner when you need something to warm you up.

¾ cup dried chickpeas (about 5 oz), picked through for dirt and stones, and soaked overnight

8 cups water

One 3-inch cinnamon stick

1 bay leaf

3 thin coins of peeled fresh ginger

Spice Mixture (recipe follows)

1½ Tbsp extra-virgin olive oil

1 large yellow onion, chopped (about 2 cups)

Salt and pepper

1 Tbsp minced garlic

1½ Tbsp grated fresh ginger

½ cup red wine

1 medium carrot, diced (about ¾ cup)

2 celery ribs, diced (about ¾ cup)

1 medium zucchini, diced (about 1 cup)

1 (14½-oz) can tomatoes, chopped, including the juice

2 or 3 Tbsp chopped fresh cilantro

*Spice Mixture*

½ Tbsp cumin seed

½ Tbsp coriander seed

¼ tsp mustard seeds

¼ tsp ground cinnamon

¼ tsp powdered turmeric

Pinch of cayenne pepper

*See instructions on next page >*

### Moroccan Chickpea Soup *continued...*

*To make soup*: Drain and rinse the chickpeas. Place them in a soup pot with the water, cinnamon stick, bay leaf, and ginger coins. Bring to a boil, lower the heat and simmer, covered, until completely tender, about 1½ hours. (Keep the chickpeas in their broth.) Meanwhile, make the Spice Mixture.

While the chickpeas are cooking, heat the oil in a large sauté pan and add the onions, ¼ teaspoon salt, and a pinch of pepper. Cook over medium heat until they begin to soften, 3 to 4 minutes. Add the garlic, grated ginger, and Spice Mixture and cook until onions are completely soft, about 3 minutes. Add the wine and cook until the pan is nearly dry, about 3 minutes. Stir in the carrots, celery, and zucchini, ¼ teaspoon salt, and a pinch of pepper and cook for 4 minutes. Add the tomatoes and simmer for 5 minutes, until vegetables are tender.

Remove the cinnamon, bay leaf, and ginger coins from the chickpeas. Add the vegetable mixture and simmer for 15 to 20 minutes. Adjust the seasoning with salt and pepper, and add the cilantro just before serving.

*To make spice mixture*: Toast the cumin and coriander seeds together in a small skillet over medium heat until fragrant, 1 to 2 minutes. Grind them in a spice grinder. Toast the mustard seeds over medium heat in the skillet until they begin to pop. Combine the spices in a small bowl and set aside.

*Tip:* You can toast the spice mixture and cook the chickpeas a day ahead of time. Just be sure to remove the cinnamon, ginger coins, and bay leaf once they're cool.

# Kasha Pilaf

*Serves 4*

**Kevin Archer**
*Catskill Animal Sanctuary Compassionate Cuisine, Saugerties, NY*

*Kevin Archer has worked in many different restaurants across the United States and he was the founding director of the Compassionate Cuisine, a culinary program at Catskill Animal Sanctuary. The goal of Compassionate Cuisine is to teach people that vegan, cruelty-free food is just as good as other food.*

The toasted buckwheat groats in this pilaf provide a nutty taste and firm texture. The savory blend of mushrooms, celery, onions and carrots balance the buckwheat for a perfect fall dish. Tarragon and parsley make this appropriate for a Thanksgiving side dish, or anytime you want to enjoy a flavorful pilaf. It's especially good with roasted vegetables.

1 Tbsp extra-virgin olive oil

1/4 lb mushrooms, sliced

Salt and freshly ground black pepper

1 small onion, diced

2 celery ribs, diced

4 cloves garlic, minced

1 carrot, diced

1 cup buckwheat groats

1/4 cup white wine

1 1/3 cups vegetable stock

2 Tbsp minced fresh tarragon

2 Tbsp minced fresh Italian (flat-leaf) parsley

Grilled or roasted vegetables, for serving

Extra-virgin olive oil, for serving

Heat the oil in a heavy-bottomed saucepan over medium-high heat. Add the mushrooms, season with salt and pepper, and sauté until they release their liquid, about 10 minutes. Add onions, celery, garlic, and carrot and sauté for 5 minutes more.

Add buckwheat and sauté for another 5 minutes to toast the buckwheat. Add the white wine, stirring to scrape up the browned bits, and simmer until liquid is almost completely absorbed. Stir in the stock, season with more salt and pepper to taste, and bring to a boil. Cover, reduce heat to medium-low, and simmer for 10 to 15 minutes, until all the stock is absorbed.

Remove from heat and add the fresh tarragon and parsley. Serve with grilled or roasted vegetables and a drizzle of olive oil.

# Roasted Parsnips & Carrots

Serves 4

### Ina Garten
*From the cookbook "Barefoot Contessa Back to Basics"*

*Ina Garten is the author of 10 cookbooks, the former owner of the Barefoot Contessa specialty food store, a permanent host on the Food Network, and a monthly food columnist. She had no formal culinary training and relied on intuition and feedback from family, friends, and customers to adjust her recipes.*

Parsnips may look like white carrots, but they actually have a very different flavor. It's similarly sweet but much earthier and even a bit spiced, almost like cinnamon. Combining them with familiar carrots made it easier for us to want to give them a try, and we're so glad we did.

- 2 lbs parsnips, peeled
- 1 lb carrots, peeled
- 3 Tbsp extra-virgin olive oil
- 1 Tbsp kosher salt
- 1½ tsp freshly ground black pepper
- 2 Tbsp minced fresh dill or parsley

Preheat the oven to 425 degrees F. If the parsnips and carrots are very thick, cut them in half lengthwise. Slice each one diagonally in 1-inch-thick slices. The vegetables will shrink while cooking, so don't make the pieces too small.

Place the cut vegetables on a sheet pan. Add the olive oil, salt, and pepper and toss well. Roast for 20 to 40 minutes, depending on the size of the vegetables, tossing occasionally, until the parsnips and carrots are just tender. Sprinkle with dill and serve hot.

*Note:* Choose topped carrots (with their greens attached) and parsnips that are white and firm to the touch.

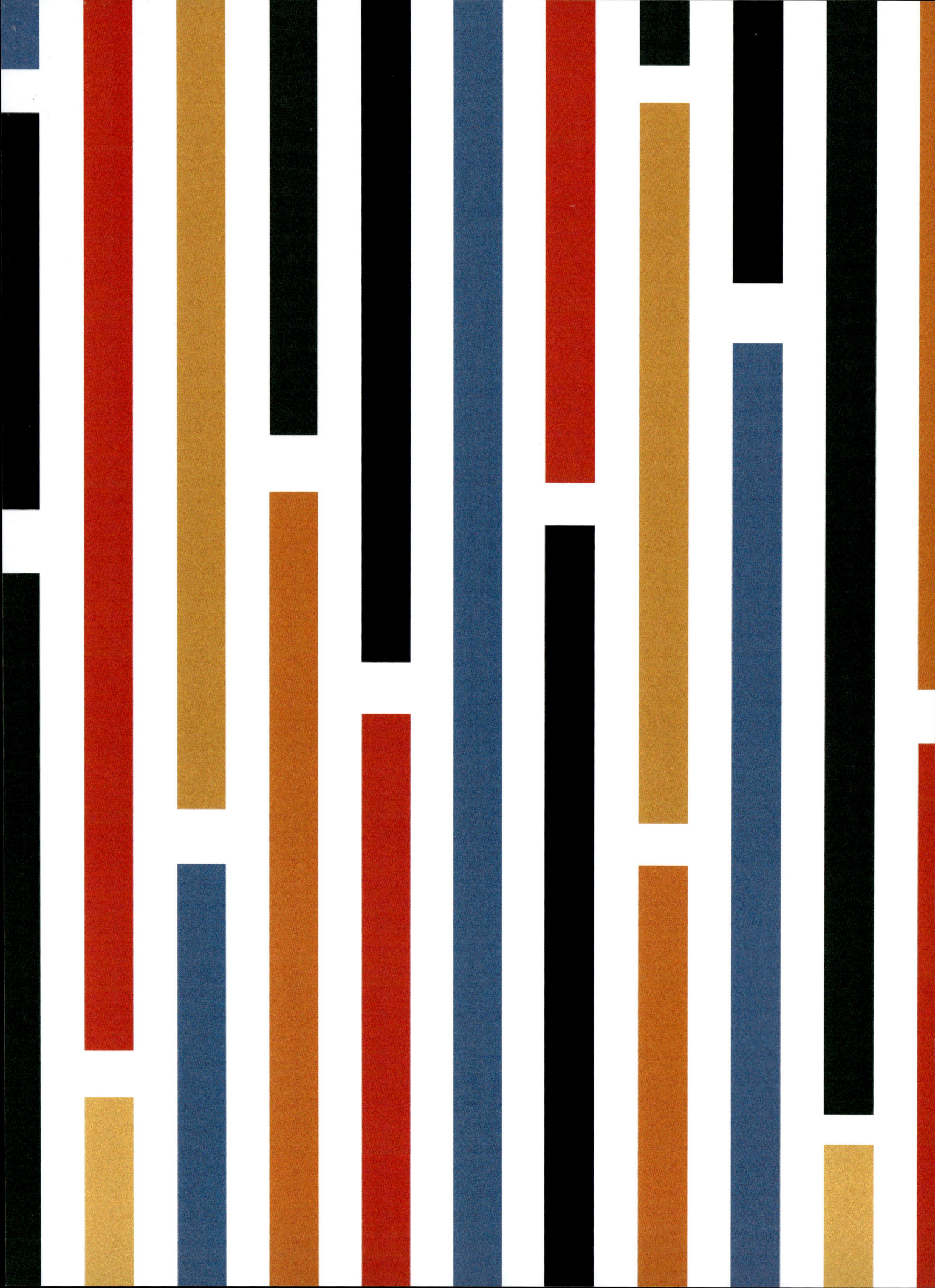

Chapter 4
# Main Dishes

The main course dishes in this cookbook range from familiar mac and cheese to flavorful soba noodles slathered in a smooth sesame sauce. The collection of recipes is delectable and there's truly something for everyone. Because we collected recipes from many different chefs, no two recipes have the same style or flavor. If you ask us, that's what makes this chapter so fun.

# Soba Sensation

*Serves 6*

**Leslie McEachern**
*Angelica Kitchen, NYC*

*Angelica Kitchen, in New York City, is a vegan restaurant. At least 95% of the ingredients they use are organically grown. They work to keep their meal prices reasonably low, and their food quality high by creating relationships with local farmers and food artisans. They care about the earth, and use all renewable energy sources and a compost to keep waste production to a minimum*

If you are in the mood for a rich and delicious meal, then this is the dish for you. These soba noodles, slathered in a sesame sauce, are delectable. And since it's served cold, it's perfect on a summer evening or tucked into a lunch box. Try adding shaved or grated carrots, shredded cabbage or wilted spinach. The sauce is so versatile, it can be served with steamed vegetables, tofu, or whole grains – or even used as a sandwich spread.

*Sauce*

1 1/3 cups tahini

1/3 cup hot water

1/3 cup brown rice vinegar

1/3 cup soy sauce

1/3 cup brown rice syrup

2 to 3 Tbsp peeled and grated ginger

2 Tbsp Dijon mustard

2 Tbsp toasted sesame oil

1 clove garlic, grated

Pinch of cayenne pepper

*For Serving*

1 (8-oz) package soba or udon noodles

1 (8-ounce) package baked tofu, cut into ½-inch cubes

1 red bell pepper, stem and seeds removed, diced

Chopped scallions, for garnish

Kimchi or sauerkraut

In a medium bowl, whisk the sauce ingredients together until smooth and creamy. (Alternatively, you can blend the ingredients in a blender or food processor.)

Cook the soba or udon noodles according to the package directions until al dente. Drain and rinse under cold running water until cold.

In a large bowl, toss the noodles, tofu and red peppers with the sauce until well coated. Divide among serving bowls and garnish with sliced scallions and kimchee or sauerkraut.

# Mushroom Popover Pie

*Serves 2-3*

**Mollie Katzen**
*From the cookbook "The Heart of the Plate"*

*Mollie Katzen is a chef, cookbook author, and artist. Her bestselling cookbooks include the "Moosewood Cookbook", "The Enchanted Broccoli Forest", and "Vegetable Haven and Sunlight Café". She has been inducted into the James Beard Cookbook Hall of Fame, and is credited with moving plant-based cuisine into mainstream American eating. She was also named as one of The Five Women Who Changed the Way We Eat by Health Magazine.*

The mushroom popover pie is both beautiful and delicious, from the gorgeous golden brown color on top to the earthy flavor of the mushrooms. It has a fantastic texture as well. It's a great combination of crispy and doughy because it bakes up like a popover, but gets cut into wedges like a pie. This recipe is easily doubled if you have a second skillet.

2 Tbsp unsalted butter, divided

1/2 onion, minced (about ½ cup)

1/2 lb fresh button mushrooms, wiped clean, stemmed if necessary, and thinly sliced

About 6 medium-sized fresh shiitake mushrooms, stemmed and minced (1/4 lb)

1 clove garlic, minced

1 1/4 tsp salt

½ tsp dried thyme

Freshly ground black pepper

3 large eggs, at room temperature

1 cup unbleached flour

1 cup milk

Preheat oven to 375 degrees F.

Melt 1 tablespoon of the butter in a 9- or 10-inch cast-iron skillet over medium-low heat. Add the onion and sauté for 5 minutes, or until softened. Add the mushrooms, garlic, ¾ teaspoon salt, thyme, and a generous amount of black pepper. Cook, stirring often, for about 15 minutes, or until the liquid the mushrooms have given off evaporates, and the mushrooms are becoming golden brown around the edges.

Meanwhile, in a blender process the eggs, milk, flour, and remaining 1/2 teaspoon salt until smooth. (If you don't have a blender, whisk together in a medium-sized bowl. It's fine if the mixture has a few lumps.) Set aside.

Transfer the mushrooms to a bowl, thoroughly wash and dry the sauté pan, and return it to the stove. Add the remaining tablespoon of butter, set the heat to low, and warm the butter until it melts and begins to foam. Immediately remove the pan from the heat, and swirl to coat the pan. (Be sure to get the corners.) Add the mushrooms, spreading them into a fairly even layer, and then pour in the batter.

Bake in the center of the oven for 25 to 30 minutes, or until the popover becomes dry on top, and feels solid when touched lightly with a fingertip. (Another sign it's done: The edges will have browned and shrunk from the sides of the pan.) Serve hot or warm, cut into wedges.

---

# Talia's Mix & Match Pesto

*Serves 6*

### Talia's Favorite Family Recipe

Talia takes a classic basil- and pine-nut pesto and breaks it down into an infinitely customizable formula (Green leaves + cheese + oil + salt), so she can use whatever ingredients she has on hand. Follow her lead and make your own signature pesto. You can toss it with whatever pasta you like, or slather it on grilled bread and top with veggies like grilled zucchini or blistered cherry tomatoes. You can even add it to vinaigrette.

1 to 2 handfuls fresh leafy green herbs
*such as basil, Italian (flat-leaf) parsley, mint, arugula (choose one or a mix).*

1 to 2 cups shredded aged hard cheese
*Such as Parmesan, Romano or Manchego (choose one or a mix).*

½ to 1 cup extra-virgin olive oil or grapeseed oil

Salt to taste

*Optional Ingredients*

1 to 2 garlic cloves

1 to 2 handfuls toasted nuts,
*Such as pinenuts, walnuts, etc.*

A splash of acidity
*Such as fresh lemon juice or flavorful vinegar.*

Pulse all ingredients together in a food processor, adding the larger amount of oil depending on how many cups of greens and cheese you used, until the pesto is a loose, almost saucy consistency. Taste often and adjust with more salt, pepper, acidity, or other ingredients.

Served tossed with cooked pasta, or spread on grilled bread.

# Lime Tofu Wraps

Serves 4-6

**George Schaller**
*Primatologist, Museum of Natural History, NYC*

*Although he is not a chef and has never run a restaurant, George Schaller has done so much for wildlife conservation that he is a natural to include in a cookbook focused on helping animals. Dr. Schaller's work has led to the creation of numerous protected parks around the world and he is often considered the 'father of wildlife conservation.'*

This is a wonderful meal that combines delicious spices and flavors. Plain tofu gets a kick of spice from coriander, cumin and paprika, and a tangy tzatziki sauce livens things up even more.

1 14-oz block firm tofu

1 Tbsp ground coriander

1 Tbsp ground cumin

1/2 tsp paprika

1/4 tsp cayenne (or more if you want more heat)

2 tsp granulated sugar

1 tsp salt

3 Tbsp peanut or canola oil (divided)

2 Tbsp fresh lime juice (about 1 lime), plus more for serving

1 onion, halved, cut into ¼-inch slices

1 to 2 red bell peppers, seeds and stems removed, cut into ¼-inch slices

2 cloves garlic, minced

4 to 6 flour tortillas, warmed (*see note*)

1 cup grated smoked cheddar cheese (or whatever cheese you prefer)

1 cup tzatziki (store-bought, or see below)

1/2 cup chopped fresh cilantro (optional)

Line a plate with several layers of paper towel. Set the tofu on the towels and place a plate on top. Weight it with a heavy can to help press out the excess liquid. Let sit for 10 minutes. Cut the tofu into ½-inch-thick slabs.

In a large bowl combine the coriander, cumin, paprika, cayenne, sugar and salt. Stir in one tablespoon of the oil and the lime juice. Add the tofu and gently toss to coat. Allow to marinate for at least 30 minutes or refrigerate and marinate for up to a day.

*Recipe continued on next page >*

### **Lime Tofu Wraps** continued...

Heat 1 tablespoon of the oil in a large skillet over medium-high heat. Add the onion and bell peppers and sauté until beginning to brown around the edges, about 5 minutes. Add the garlic and cook 1 minute more. Transfer to a plate.

Clean the sauté pan and return to medium-high heat. Add the remaining tablespoon of oil and heat until shimmering. Add the tofu (reserve the marinade) and fry until crispy and golden, about 5 to 7 minutes. Add the marinade and cook until mostly absorbed. Squeeze a little extra lime juice in at the end.

Divide the tofu and sautéed vegetables among the warm tortillas. Top with grated cheese, tzatziki and cilantro. Fold the top and bottom edges up, roll into a burrito, and serve.

*Note:* To warm the tortillas, wrap in foil and heat in a 350 degree F oven for 20 minutes. Or warm them one by one in a dry hot skillet for a minute or two each side, wrapping in foil to keep warm as you go.

*Tzatziki*

1 (17.5-oz) container plain whole milk Greek yogurt

1 English cucumber, seeded and diced

3 cloves garlic, minced, or more to taste

2 Tbsp extra-virgin olive oil

Juice of ½ lemon, or more to taste

½ tsp dried dill

Salt, to taste

*Makes 3 cups*

Mix all ingredients in a medium bowl. Taste and adjust seasonings if desired.

# Aunt Debbie's Artichoke Lasagna

Serves 8

**Maeve's Favorite Family Recipe**

"This recipe is the perfect blend of sophistication and comfort food," says Maeve. "The white sauce and cheese are balanced by the tangy artichokes and earthy lasagna. This dish is great for a cold winter night, but delicate enough for warm seasons as well. A quick green salad and garlic bread can complete the meal."

*Filling*

2 Tbsp unsalted butter

1 lb mushrooms, sliced

3 garlic cloves, minced

2 (8-oz) packages frozen artichoke hearts, thawed, coarsely chopped (use canned or bottled if you cannot find frozen)

*White Sauce*

4 ½ Tbsp unsalted butter

4 1/2 Tbsp all-purpose flour

4 1/2 cups lowfat or whole milk

2 1/2 cups (about 7 1/2 oz) freshly grated Parmesan cheese, divided

Ground nutmeg

1 (9-oz) package oven-ready (no-boil) lasagna noodles

1 lb whole-milk mozzarella cheese, thinly sliced

*To make the filling:* Melt butter in large skillet over medium-high heat. Add mushrooms and garlic and sauté until they release their juices and begin to brown, about 7 minutes. Add artichokes and cook until liquid is evaporated, stirring occasionally. Season with salt and pepper to taste.

*To make the white sauce:* Melt butter in medium saucepan over medium-high heat. Add flour and stir to make a paste (this is called a roux). Cook, stirring, for 1 minute. Gradually whisk in milk, a little at a time, letting the roux absorb the liquid before adding more. Reduce heat to medium and simmer until the sauce thickens, stirring occasionally, about 20 minutes. Stir in 1 1/2 cups of the Parmesan. Season to taste with salt, pepper, and ground nutmeg.

*To assemble:* Preheat oven to 350 degrees F. Spread 2/3 cup white sauce over the bottom of 13- by 9-inch glass baking dish. Top with enough noodles to cover bottom of dish. Spread 1/4 of the artichoke mixture over the noodles. Spoon 2/3 cup white sauce over the artichoke layer. Top the white sauce with 1/4 of the mozzarella. Sprinkle with 3 tablespoons Parmesan. Top with enough noodles to cover. Repeat, layering 3 more times, finishing with a layer of noodles, then the remaining white sauce. Sprinkle with the remaining Parmesan.

Cover lasagna with foil and bake for 1 hour. Remove the foil and increase temperature to 450 degrees F. Bake lasagna until golden on top, about 10 minutes longer.

# Vegetarian Angel Hair Pasta

*Serves 6*

**Jane Goodall**
*The Jane Goodall Institute*

*Jane Goodall is a primatologist, ethologist, anthropologist, and UN Messenger of Peace. She is the founder of the Jane Goodall Institute and the Roots and Shoots organization, which aims to empower and encourage youth to pursue their passion, make a difference, and become leaders for the next generation.*

Angel Hair Pasta is definitely a crowd pleaser. Almost all of the tasters who tried this recipe (including the picky eaters) agree that this is a delicious recipe. The sauce is a delectable combination of vegetables and herbs that will make your mouth water for more.

3 Tbsp extra-virgin olive oil

1 medium onion, diced

1 medium eggplant, cut into ½ inch cubes

2 portobello mushrooms, stems removed, roughly chopped

2 cloves garlic, minced

1 (28-oz) can diced tomatoes (or 3 ½ cups peeled and diced fresh tomatoes)

1/4 cup chopped fresh Italian (flat-leaf) parsley

1/4 cup chopped fresh basil

Salt and freshly ground black pepper, to taste

8 oz angel hair pasta

Grated Parmesan cheese, for serving

Heat the oil in a large sauté pan over medium heat. Add the onions and sauté until soft, about 7 minutes. Reduce heat to medium-low and add the eggplant and mushrooms. Sauté until soft, about 10 minutes. Add the garlic and sauté 1 minute more.

Add the tomatoes and continue to cook over low heat for ages (about 30 minutes). If the mixture becomes dry, add a little water. Stir in the chopped fresh herbs and season with salt and pepper to taste.

Meanwhile, bring a large pot of water to a boil and salt generously. Cook the pasta in the boiling salted water according to the package instructions, until al dente. Drain.

Return the cooked pasta to the empty pot and add the sauce. Toss to coat. Divide pasta among plates and serve sprinkled with Parmesan cheese.

# Idaho Chili

*Serves 4*

**Maren Jackson**
*Seva Restaurant, Ann Arbor, MI*

*Maren and Jeff Jackson run the vegetarian Seva Restaurant, with locations in Ann Arbor and Detroit, Michigan. The restaurant offers a diverse menu that attracts both vegetarians and omnivores, and they aim to provide both novel options and comfort food to meet any diner preference.*

Although it doesn't have meat and tons of heat like most chilis, this kid-friendly version doesn't lack in flavor at all. In fact, it gets its name because it's made with things they grow in Idaho. If you don't want to soak dried chickpeas, you can use a 15-ounce can.

- ¼ cup dried chickpeas
- 2 Tbsp extra-virgin olive oil
- 3 cloves garlic, minced
- 1 ½ cups vegetable stock or water
- ½ cup dried brown or green lentils
- 1 large potato, diced (¼ lb; about 2 cups)
- 1 onion, diced (1 ½ cups)
- 2 carrots, diced (1 ½ cups)
- 1 cup sliced celery
- 1 cup tomato sauce
- 1 cup diced tomatoes
- 1 tsp chili powder
- 1/2 tsp ground cumin
- 1/3 tsp oregano
- 1/8 tsp cayenne
- 1/2 tsp salt
- 1/4 tsp pepper

*For Serving*

Chopped scallions or white onion, diced avocado, sour cream and/or shredded cheddar cheese

Rinse and pick through the chickpeas for stones or debris. Place in a medium bowl, cover with water and soak for 3 to 4 hours, or overnight. After soaking, discard the soaking water, rinse the chickpeas well and drain. (Alternatively you can use a 15-ounce can of chickpeas, drained and rinsed.)

Heat the olive oil in a 3-quart saucepan over medium heat. Add the garlic and sauté until fragrant, about 1 minute. Add the the soaked (or canned) chickpeas and vegetable stock or water. Cover, bring to a simmer over high heat, reduce to medium-low, and cook for 1 hour.

Add the lentils, potatoes, onions, carrots and celery. Bring to a simmer and cook until beans and vegetables are tender, about 30 to 40 minutes.

Add the tomato sauce, diced tomatoes, chili powder, cumin, oregano, cayenne, salt and pepper. Bring to a simmer and cook for 30 minutes. Taste and adjust seasonings if desired.

Ladle chili into bowls and pass desired toppings at the table.

---

# Grandpa Eastman's Macaroni & Cheese

*Serves 8*

### McKenzie Tell's Favorite Family Recipe

This mac and cheese is McKenzie's favorite because it's bursting with flavor thanks to garlic, onions and a generous helping of grated extra-sharp cheddar cheese. Once you have this version, you'll never want the boxed stuff again.

1 medium yellow onion, finely chopped

5 cloves garlic, minced

4 Tbsp (½ stick) unsalted butter

4 Tbsp all-purpose flour

2 cups whole milk

1 tsp salt

2 cups grated Tillamook Vintage Extra Sharp White Cheddar cheese

1 lb elbow macaroni noodles

Paprika

Preheat oven to 350 degrees F. Bring a large pot of water to a boil and salt generously. Add the macaroni and boil according to the package instructions. Drain.

Meanwhile, melt the butter in a large sauté pan over medium-high heat. Add the onion and sauté until softened, about 5 minutes. Add the garlic and sauté until fragrant, about 1 minute more.

Add the flour, stirring to make a paste (this is called a roux), and allow to cook, stirring frequently, for 1 minute. Add the milk a little at a time, allowing the roux to absorb the liquid before adding more. Remove from heat and season with salt to taste.

Layer half the cooked macaroni in a 9-by-13-inch casserole dish. Top with half the cheese. Add the remaining macaroni and top with the remaining cheese. Pour the white sauce evenly over the top. Sprinkle with paprika. Bake for 30 minutes, until cheese is melted and sauce is bubbly.

# Quinoa & Chickpea Burgers with Avocado Mayo

*Serves 4*

**Jaco Smith**
*Lechon Restaurant, Portland*

*Born and raised in South Africa, Jaco fell in love with elaborate meals and flavors by cooking alongside his mother on the family's cattle, sheep and grain farm. Inspired by his mother's large 'themed' meals, Jaco began to explore ingredients and tastes from around the world. This passion led to a love of South American cuisine and eventually to opening Lechon, a South American fusion restaurant along the banks of the Willamette River in Portland.*

One may think that nothing can come close to a traditional beef burger, but this recipe proves that wrong. It has a unique twist by using a chickpea and chipotle paste as a base ingredient. The crispy patty and juicy tomato on a lightly toasted bun is spectacular. This dish pairs nicely with a slice of fresh feta. It does have a slight kick to it due to the chipotles. For less spice, do not add as many chipotles, or none at all.

*Chickpea Burgers*

½ cup quinoa

1 cup water or broth

3 Tbsp extra-virgin olive oil (divided)

1 medium red onion, diced

3 cloves garlic, minced

1 (15-oz) can drained and rinsed chickpeas (or 2 cups cooked)

3 canned chipotles in adobo

1 red bell pepper, minced

1 bunch fresh cilantro or fresh Italian (flat-leaf) parsley, chopped

1 cup chickpea flour

1 Tbsp salt

Freshly ground pepper

*Avocado Mayo*

2 avocados

3 Tbsp extra-virgin olive oil

2 Tbsp fresh lemon juice

2 Tbsp water

½ tsp sea salt

*For Serving*

4 hamburger buns, toasted

4 thick slices feta cheese

Crispy lettuce, tomatoes, pickles and sliced onions

*See instructions on next page >*

**Quinoa & Chickpea Burgers with Avocado Mayo** *continued...*

*To make the chickpea burgers:* In a medium saucepan, combine the quinoa and water or broth. Cover and bring to a boil over medium-high heat. Reduce to low and cook until fluffy and liquid is absorbed, about 15 minutes. Remove from heat and allow to cool. You should have 1 ½ cups of quinoa (if you have more, reserve it for another use).

Heat 1 tablespoon of the oil in a large sauté pan or cast iron skillet. Add the onion and sauté until beginning to brown around the edges. Add the garlic and sauté about 1 minute more.

In a food processor, process the chickpeas and chipotles until they form a slightly textured paste (be sure to stop occasionally and scrape down the sides of the bowl). Transfer to a large bowl. Add the cooked quinoa, sautéed onions, red peppers, herbs and chickpea flour; mix to combine. Season with salt and pepper to taste. Transfer to an airtight container and refrigerate for at least 1 hour to firm up the mixture and allow the flavors to meld.

Divide the mixture into 4 equal-sized balls, then form into patties.

Heat the remaining 2 tablespoons of olive oil in a large sauté pan or cast iron skillet over medium-high heat. Add the patties and cook until browned, about 5 minutes. Turn and cook the other side until browned, about 5 minutes more.

*To make the avocado mayo:* Cut the avocado in half and remove the pit. Scoop out the flesh into a blender and add the olive oil, lemon juice, water and salt. Blend for 30 seconds until smooth and creamy. Spoon into a glass jar and store in fridge until needed.

*To serve:* Toast the buns and spread with avocado mayo. Add the chickpea patties, top with feta and the desired accompaniments.

# Creamy Mac N Cheeze

*Serves 6*

**Heidi Lovig**
*Heidi Ho Organics, Portland, OR*

*Heidi Lovig is a trained chef from Portland, OR, who appeared on the entrepreneurial reality show "Shark Tank" to promote her organic line of plant-based "cheezes". Her organic "cheeze" ingredients include cashews, vegetables, and herbs and do not rely on starch, fat, or other unpronounceable fillers. As a chef, Heidi is "fanatic" about farm-to-table, sustainable, and seasonal dining.*

Who doesn't love a warm bowl of mac and cheese? Normally, not everyone can have this delicious meal because of the dairy. But this recipe turns the meal into one everyone can enjoy by using Heidi Ho's delicious vegan cheese instead of traditional cheese. Some people are skeptical about vegan substitutes, but this one is particularly good.

16 oz elbow macaroni

1/4 cup unsweetened soy creamer

2 Tbsp Vegan Butter (Earth Balance)

1 tsp salt

1 (10-oz) package Heidi Ho Creamy Chia Cheeze

Fill a large stock pot with about 4 cups of water, and bring to boil. Add in Macaroni and reduce heat to medium and cover. Continue to cook for about 10 minutes, until the macaroni is soft.

In a smaller sauce pan, melt the vegan butter down over medium heat and add the soy creamer, salt and mix well. Let cook for about 4 minutes.

Add the Heidi Ho Creamy Chia Cheeze to the butter mixture and stir well. Continue to cook on medium heat until sauce is nice and warm.

Drain the cooked noodles, and place them back into the stock pot, removing from heat. Pour in cheeze sauce and mix well, making sure every last noodle is covered.

Serve in a bowl, or as a side dish.

# Sweet Potato Coconut Curry

Serves 6

**Becky Atkins**
*Stella Taco, Portland, OR*

*Becky Atkins is the co-owner of Stella Taco in Portland, Oregon. Their food is Texan-influenced food and is inspired by the time she and her husband lived in the Lone Star State.*

This mouthwatering dish with warm spices is great for a cozy winter night. With a hint of curry and a splash of sweet coconut milk to balance out the flavor, it is the perfect meal to spice up your day. It's not served at Stella Taco, one of our favorite taco places in Portland, but owner Becky Atkins shared it with us because it's a favorite in her home kitchen. Now it's a favorite of ours, too.

1 Tbsp extra-virgin olive oil

1 large onion, roughly chopped

3 carrots, roughly chopped

1 jalapeño, seeded and chopped

3 cloves garlic, minced

1 Tbsp curry powder

2 tsp ground coriander

2 tsp ground ginger

2 tsp smoked paprika

1 tsp cayenne

2 Tbsp Thai yellow curry paste

2 roasted red bell peppers (from a jar), drained and chopped

1 large sweet potato, peeled and cut into ½-inch cubes

2 (14-oz) cans coconut milk

32 oz vegetable broth

1 bunch fresh cilantro, plus more for garnish

2 Tbsp fresh lime juice

Pinch of sugar, as needed

Kosher salt, to taste

1 large zucchini, cut into ½-inch cubes

1 head cauliflower, separated into small florets

1 cup grape tomatoes

Steamed rice, for serving

Heat the oil in a large sauté pan over medium-high heat. Add the onion, carrots, and jalapeño. Saute until tender and onion begins to caramelize, about 10 minutes. Add the garlic and saute 1 minute more.

Clear the vegetables to one side of the pan and add the curry powder, coriander, ginger, smoked paprika and cayenne. Allow spices to toast for 2 to 3 minutes. Stir into the vegetables and add the curry paste.

Add the red bell peppers, sweet potato, coconut milk, and veggie stock. Cover, bring to a simmer, reduce heat to medium-low and cook at a gentle simmer for 30 to 45 minutes.

Transfer mixture to a blender and add 1/2 bunch of cilantro, salt, and lime juice. Set the lid to the blender ajar and cover with a dish towel (this will allow the steam to escape while blending; otherwise the steam will build up and the lid could explode off and spray the hot contents everywhere). Blend until smooth. Taste and add a touch of sugar to balance spice and sweetness, or add more lime juice or salt.

Return mixture to the pot and set over medium-low heat. Add the diced zucchini, grape tomatoes and cauliflower. Cook until vegetables are just tender, about 15-20 minutes.

Serve curry over steamed jasmine or basmati rice and garnish with cilantro leaves.

# Chili Verde

*Serves 8*

**Eric Bell**
*Standing Stone Brewing Co., Ashland, OR*

*Eric Bell is the head chef at Standing Stone Brewery in Ashland, Oregon. The food there reflects his devotion to using local, sustainable food. They hide nothing about how their beef and lamb is produced; customers can even go on a tour to view Standing Stone's farm. They work with local farmers to ensure high quality food.*

This tomatillo-packed twist on traditional chilli is fantastic. It's perfect the day you make it, but also makes great leftovers. Although it has green chiles and other strong spices, it's surprisingly mild. Feel free to increase the spice level to your preference with hot sauce or cayenne pepper.

1 Tbsp extra-virgin olive oil

2 large yellow onions, cut into ½-inch dice

4 large cloves garlic, minced

2 quarts vegetable stock

2 (12-oz) cans crushed tomatillos, or fresh equivalent

1 (12-oz) can diced green chiles, or fresh equivalent (roasted, peeled and diced)

¼ cup chopped fresh cilantro

Salt and freshly ground black pepper to taste

2 Tbsp vegetable oil

2 (8-oz) packages tempeh, cut into 1-inch cubes

For Serving

2 cups grated Monterey Jack cheese

2 large tomatoes, cut into ½-inch dice

16 corn tortillas, warmed, or 8 cups steamed rice

Heat a large pot or Dutch oven over medium-high heat. Add the oil and heat until shimmering. Add the onions and sauté until softened and beginning to brown, about 20 minutes. Add the garlic and sauté about 1 minute more. Add the stock, stir in the tomatillos, green chilies, cilantro, and salt and pepper to taste. Bring to a simmer and cook until the liquid is reduced by one third.

Meanwhile, heat a large sauté pan over medium-high heat. Add the vegetable oil and heat until shimmering. Add the tempeh and fry until golden brown and crisp, 4 to 5 minutes on each side. Use tongs or a slotted spoon to transfer the tempeh to the paper-towel-lined plate to drain.

When ready to serve, divide the fried tempeh among bowls. Ladle chili verde on top and sprinkle with cheese. Garnish with diced tomatoes. Serve with tortillas or rice on the side.

# Skillet Spanakopita

Serves 4-6

**Mark Bittman**
*From the cookbook "How to Cook Everything Fast"*

*Mark Bittman has written over a dozen popular books, a few of which have been turned into successful apps. He has written many books such as "How to Cook Everything Fast," "How to Cook Everything Vegetarian," and "How to Cook Everything Thanksgiving." He believes that the food that we eat and buy can make or break our health and the health of the planet.*

If you haven't had spanikopita before, this one's definitely worth a try. It's a spinach and cheese pie with a deliciously crispy topping. Once you make this recipe, we think you'll agree with us—it's hard to get enough of it. Mark Bittman says, "This skillet spanakopita preserves all the flavors and textures of the classic dish but eliminates much of the busywork."

10 to 12 sheets phyllo dough, thawed in the refrigerator

3 Tbsp extra-virgin olive oil

4 scallions

2 (10-oz) bags spinach

Salt and pepper

2 eggs

6 oz feta cheese (1 1/2 cups crumbled)

1 tsp dried dill

1/4 tsp nutmeg

4 Tbsp (1/2 stick) butter

Heat the oven to 350 degrees F. On a dry surface, cut the phyllo into thin shreds.

Heat the olive oil in a medium ovenproof skillet over low heat. Trim and chop the scallions and the spinach.

Raise the heat to medium-high and add the scallions and spinach, a handful at a time; sprinkle with salt and pepper. Cook, stirring frequently until the spinach leaves are just wilted, 2 or 3 minutes after the last addition.

Meanwhile, crack the eggs into a medium bowl and beat them. Crumble 1 1/2 cups feta and add to the bowl. Add 1 teaspoon dill and 1/4 teaspoon nutmeg. Melt 4 tablespoons butter in the microwave or in a small pot over medium-low heat.

When the spinach is wilted, stir in the egg and feta mixture and sprinkle the shredded phyllo dough over the top. Drizzle the melted butter over the phyllo.

Bake until the phyllo is crisp, about 30 minutes. Cut the pie into wedges and serve hot, warm, or at room temperature.

# Spinach Stuffed Portobello Bowls

*Serves 4*

**Danielle Premo**
*Minirette, Seattle, WA*

*Danielle Premo is a chef and cooking instructor who likes to introduce people to vegetables, grains and legumes that complement a balanced diet. She has a passion for building community through food, and offers personalized catering, menu-planning, and chef work through Minirette in Seattle, WA.*

These delectable portobello mushrooms are filled with a flavorful mix of cashews, sautéed leeks and spinach, and are sure to please your dinner guests. They are very simple and don't take long to make. It's a great first course or main course that can be made ahead of time. Just reheat in the oven when you are ready to serve them.

½ cup raw cashews, soaked in cold water for two hours

3 Tbsp coconut oil

2 leeks, diced

1 1/2 tsp salt (divided)

¼ tsp freshly ground black pepper

2 cups fresh spinach leaves

3 Tbsp balsamic vinegar

1 Tbsp extra-virgin olive oil

1 tsp tamari or soy sauce

4 portobello mushrooms, stems removed

2 roasted red peppers, sliced, for garnish

Drain the soaked cashews, add to a food processor and pulse until finely chopped.

Heat the coconut oil in a large sauté pan over medium heat. Add the leeks, ½ teaspoon of the salt and pepper. Sauté for 3 to 5 minutes, until leeks are tender. Add the chopped cashews and sauté for 1 to 2 minutes. Add the spinach and balsamic vinegar and cook until the spinach is wilted. Cover with a lid, reduce heat to low and keep warm.

In a small bowl, mix together the olive oil, tamari and remaining teaspoon salt. Heat a large skillet over medium-high heat. Brush the tamari mixture onto each mushroom and sear in the hot pan, gill side down, for 5 minutes. Flip the mushrooms over and fill with the sautéed leeks and spinach. Cover the pan with a lid and let cook an additional 5 minutes. Serve warm with a garnish of sliced roasted red pepper.

# Alboronia (Ratatouille)

*Serves 6*

**Ángel Custodio Ruiz**
*Enrique Becerra, Seville Spain*

*Luis Hernandez and Ángel Custodio Ruiz work at Enrique Becerra in Seville, Spain. The food there is all based on Southern Spanish cuisine. They use high-quality, local ingredients to make the food place-based and authentic.*

Alboronia is a recipe of Arabic origin very similar to French ratatouille. According to tradition it was offered during the wedding of sultan Al Mamun. Today it is a very common dish in Andalucia, a region in Southern Spain, where it was introduced by the Arabs more than a thousand years ago. Serve this with couscous for a tasty late-summer meal.

4 to 5 Tbsp extra-virgin olive oil, divided

1 eggplant, cut into 1-inch cubes

Salt and freshly ground black pepper

1 zucchini, cut into 1-inch cubes

1 onion, diced

1 green bell pepper, ribs and seeds removed, diced

3 cloves garlic, minced

1 tsp smoked paprika

1 Tbsp sherry or red wine vinegar

1 (15-oz can) diced tomatoes

1 ½ lbs winter squash
*Such as butternut squash, peeled and cut into 1-inch cubes (about 2 cups).*

Couscous or crusty bread, for serving

Heat 2 to 3 tablespoons of the olive oil in a Dutch oven over medium-high heat. Add the eggplant, season with salt and pepper, and sauté until tender and browned, about 7 minutes. Transfer to a large bowl.

Heat another tablespoon of oil in the pot and add the zucchini. Season with salt and pepper and sauté until tender, about five minutes. Transfer to the bowl with the eggplant.

Heat the remaining tablespoon of oil in the pot and add the onion and peppers. Season with salt and pepper. Sauté until softened, about 7 minutes. Add the garlic and sauté 1 minute more.

Return the eggplant and zucchini to the pot, along with the squash, paprika, vinegar and tomatoes. Bring to a simmer, taste and adjust seasonings with more salt, pepper, paprika or vinegar if desired. Reduce heat to medium-low, cover and cook until squash is tender, about 15 minutes. Serve with couscous.

**Chapter 5**

# Desserts

We couldn't leave out dessert! It's so universally loved — especially by us. This chapter contains a variety of different sweet treats. There are delicious homemade Almond Joy candies, and Apple Cakes that are basically miniature apple pies. Unlike some dessert recipes that take forever to make, these were all pretty quick and easy.

# French Apple Cakes

*Serves 8*

**Papa Haydn Restaurant**
Portland, OR

*Papa Haydn restaurant in Portland has been a staple for nearly 40 years and is known throughout the region for its incredible desserts. A family run restaurant, their locally sourced meals and recipes often take advantage of the Pacific Northwest's wide assortment of delicious fruits.*

For this dessert, the chefs at Papa Haydn adapted cookbook author Dorie Greenspan's French Apple Cake and turned it into adorable mini apple pies. They're bursting with flavor, from the soft baked apple to the assortment of spices such as cinnamon and nutmeg. To finish off these delightful treats, add a dollop of whipped cream.

1 ½ cups all-purpose flour

1 ½ tsp baking powder

¼ tsp salt

4 eggs, at room temperature

1 ½ cups granulated sugar

6 Tbsp dark rum

1 tsp vanilla extract

1 cup (2 sticks) unsalted butter, melted and cooled

8 apples, peeled, cored and cut into ½-inch chunks

Powdered sugar, for dusting

Preheat oven to 300 degrees F. Grease eight 8-ounce ramekins with butter.

In a small bowl, whisk together the flour, baking powder and salt.

With a standing mixer or using a hand-held mixer, beat the eggs on medium-high speed until foamy. Beat in the sugar, rum and vanilla until well combined. Reduce speed to low and add half of the flour mixture, mixing until incorporated. Mix in half the melted butter. Repeat with the remaining flour and butter. Fold in the apples.

Divide mixture among the prepared ramekins, filling all the way to the top (the cakes will not rise). Set the ramekins on a baking sheet.

Bake for about 40 minutes, turning the baking sheet from front to back halfway through.

Allow to cool. Run a knife along the inside of the ramekins to loosen the cakes. Invert onto serving plates. Dust the tops with powdered sugar and serve.

# Carrot Cake with Cream Cheese Frosting

*Serves 12*

**Willa's Favorite Family Recipe**

This carrot cake is packed full of carrots, raisins, and nuts so it's not too unhealthy, right? But aside from that, it's just a delicious treat in general. The cake is moist, sweet, and earthy, and the rich cream-cheese frosting compliments the cake. Feel free to leave out the nuts or raisins if you like, but we think it's not the same without them. Great for parties and whenever else you need a scrumptious dessert.

*Cake*

4 eggs

2 cups granulated sugar

1 ¼ cups extra-virgin olive oil

2 tsp vanilla extract

2 cups all-purpose flour

2 tsp baking soda

2 tsp baking powder

½ tsp salt

1 Tbsp ground cinnamon

4 cups packed grated carrots

1 cup chopped pecans or walnuts

1 cup raisins

*Cream Cheese Frosting*

½ cup butter, softened

8 oz cream cheese, softened

2 cups powdered sugar

1 tsp vanilla extract

1 cup chopped pecans or walnuts

*To make cake:* Preheat oven to 350 degrees F. Grease and flour a 9- by 13-inch pan.

In a large mixing bowl, beat together the eggs, sugar, olive oil and vanilla. Mix in flour, baking soda, baking powder, salt and cinnamon. Stir in carrots. Fold in the nuts and raisins.

Pour the batter into the prepared pan. Bake for 40 to 50 minutes, or until a toothpick inserted into the center comes out clean. Allow the cake to cool for 10 minutes in the pan, then run a knife along the edge and invert onto a wire cooling rack. Allow to cool completely before frosting with Cream Cheese Frosting.

*To make frosting:* In the bowl of a stand mixer, or using a hand mixer, beat the butter, cream cheese, powdered sugar, and vanilla until smooth and creamy. Stir in the nuts.

# Mini Key Lime Pies

*Serves 12*

**Brooke's Favorite Family Recipe**

Key Lime Pie is a great summer treat, and this vegan version is especially sweet because it's made in individual muffin tins. They're perfect for a party. Although the recipe is a bit time consuming to make because you have to squeeze limes and let the pie chill, the end product — a cool, coconutty, sweet dessert — is definitely worth the wait.

*Crust*

1/4 cups graham cracker crumbs

1/4 cup (4 Tbsp) vegan butter, melted
*Such as Earth Balance.*

*Filling*

1 cup raw cashews, soaked for 4 to 6 hours (or overnight), drained

3/4 cup light or full-fat coconut milk, well shaken

1/4 cup coconut oil, melted

Zest and juice from 3 to 4 large limes or 6 to 7 key limes (1 Tbsp zest, 1/2 cup juice)

1/3 to 1/2 cup agave nectar, to taste

*To make the crust:* Preheat oven to 375 degrees F. Line a standard muffin tin with 12 paper liners.

In a food processor, pulse the graham crackers until finely ground. Add the melted butter and pulse to combine.

Distribute the crumbs evenly among muffin tins and press with the bottom of a glass or the back of a spoon to pack down and flatten. Bake for 10 minutes or until the crumbs have darkened a bit. Remove and set aside to cool.

*To make the filling:* Place the filling ingredients in a blender or food processor and puree until creamy and smooth. Taste and adjust flavor as needed, adding more lime zest or juice for more tartness, or more agave for added sweetness.

Pour the filling into the muffin tins and tap on counter to release air bubbles. Top with a bit more lime zest and loosely cover with plastic wrap.

Freeze for 2 to 4 hours or until firm. Remove from the freezer for 10 to 15 minutes to thaw before serving. (Will keep covered in the freezer for up to 2 weeks, though they're best when fresh.)

# Peanut Butter Cookies

*Makes about 3 dozen*

**Karen Pride**
*Harlow Restaurant, Portland, OR*

*Chefs Karen Pride and Brittney Galloway are pioneering new worlds of flavor with their gluten-free, primarily vegan and largely vegetarian Harlow Restaurant. Heavily influenced by Pacific Northwest fare, their focus is on fresh and local ingredients.*

These peanut buttery vegan and gluten-free cookies are crispy and addictive. If you're looking to limit your refined sugar, this recipe fits the bill, since it's sweetened with maple syrup.

4 cups Bob's Red Mill gluten-free all-purpose flour

2 tsp baking soda

1 ½ tsp cinnamon

1 ½ tsp salt

2 cups peanut butter

2 cups maple syrup

2/3 cup coconut oil

1 Tbsp vanilla

Preheat oven to 350 degrees F. Line two rimmed baking sheets with parchment paper.

In a large mixing bowl, whisk together the flour, baking soda, cinnamon, and salt.

In a separate bowl, stir together the peanut butter, syrup, oil and vanilla until well combined.

Stir the wet ingredients into the dry until just combined. Refrigerate dough until cold, about 1 hour.

Use an ice cream scoop to portions of dough the size of golf balls. Arrange 2 inches apart on the prepared baking sheets. Press each ball with a fork in a criss-cross pattern. Bake for 11 to 12 minutes, until fully set and the cookies are golden.

Allow to cool for a few minutes on the baking sheet before using a spatula to transfer to a cooling rack.

# Rambo's Vegan Rice Crispy Treats

*Makes about 16*

**Linda Soper Kolton**
*Catskill Animal Sanctuary Compassionate Cuisine, Saugerties, NY*

*Linda Soper-Kolton is a vegan chef who started out working at a non-profit before enrolling in Manhattan's Natural Gourmet Institute for Health and Culinary Arts. After graduating, she pursued her dream of owning a café, and started GreenGourmetToGo. Then, she started teaching people how to cook healthier, by using more plants. She enrolled at the Institute of Integrative Nutrition, and earned her certification as a holistic health coach. After this, she took a job teaching cooking at the Catskill Animal Sanctuary.*

This is a yummy vegan twist on a classic kid treat. It's made with sunflower seed butter, sesame seeds and flax seeds, so it's even a bit healthy too. We'd like to warn you though: if you make this recipe, you won't be able to stop eating it. It is tasty without a doubt. The animal sanctuary that sent us the recipe says the bars were named after a sheep called Rambo. "Rambo came to Catskill Animal Sanctuary angry and unpredictable," they wrote. "Over time, and with much love and patience, Rambo showed us that he was much more than he appeared to be, just like these Rice Cripsy Treats are more than just a simple treat. They're veganized to demonstrate that we can choose compassion over cruelty in our diets and still enjoy our favorite foods."

*Crispy Treats*

4 cups rice crispy cereal

2/3 cup creamy sunflower seed butter

2/3 cup brown rice syrup

1/3 cup coconut oil, melted

1/4 cup sesame seeds

1/4 cup ground flax seeds

1 tsp vanilla extract

*Chocolate Frosting (optional)*

1 cup vegan chocolate chips

1 Tbsp coconut oil

1 Tbsp vanilla

Lightly grease a 9- by 9-inch baking pan. Pour the cereal into a large bowl. In a small saucepan over low heat, mix together the sunflower seed butter, brown rice syrup, coconut oil, sesame seeds and flax seeds. Cook, stirring, until heated through, about 3 to 5 minutes. Be careful not to let it scorch. Remove from heat and stir in vanilla. Let cool for a few minutes.

Pour the mixture over the cereal and mix until everything is coated and there are no dry spots. (Use your hands if necessary.) Pour the mixture into the prepared pan and press down firmly until flat. Place pan in refrigerator for 30 minutes or in the freezer for 15 minutes before spreading with chocolate frosting or cutting and serving.

*To make chocolate frosting:* Set a small pot with water over medium heat. Bring water to a simmer and place a metal or glass bowl over the pot. Add the chocolate chips and coconut oil to the bowl and warm until almost completely melted, stirring occasionally. Remove the bowl from heat and continue stirring to melt the remaining chips. (Alternatively, you can melt the chips and coconut oil in a microwave.) Spread the melted chocolate over the chilled Rice Crispy Treats and chill again till chocolate has hardened. Cut into bars and serve.

# Raw Chocolate Almond Joy

*Makes about 2 dozen*

**Jia Patton**
*From the cookbook "Celebrate Life!"*

*Jia Patton was the head of her own cooking school for over fourteen years. She taught the importance of using organic and local fruits and vegetables and she showed others how they could add nutrition to their diets. She is the recipe author for John Robbins's May All Be Fed, Diet for a New World.*

When you think of Almond Joy, you think of the chocolate coated coconut and almond candy. This is a great way to make your own version of your favorite candy, and it's much healthier too. This recipe is really simple, quick, and the perfect last-minute dessert.

*Chocolate Layer*

1 ½ cups raw cacao

¾ cup coconut oil, melted

1/3 cup honey or other liquid sweetener

10 drops vanilla stevia or more honey

2 tsp vanilla powder or extract

⅛ tsp sea salt

*Coconut Layer*

1 cup unsweetened shredded dry coconut

¼ cup coconut oil, melted

2 Tbsp honey or other liquid sweetener

1 tsp powdered vanilla or extract

1 pinch sea salt

18 almonds, cut in half

*To make the chocolate layers:* In a medium mixing bowl, combine all the ingredients for the chocolate layers and stir well.

*To make the coconut layer:* In a small mixing bowl, combine all the ingredients for the coconut layer and stir well.

*To assemble:* Use a square-cavity silicone candy mold and fill each cavity 1/3 of the way with the chocolate mixture until half of it has been used (be sure to save the remaining half for the top layer).

Freeze until hard. Remove the mold from the freezer. Top the chocolate layer with a small amount of the coconut mixture, pressing it in firmly. Top each candy with the remaining chocolate mixture until level with the top.

Put a ½ piece of almond on top of each chocolate. Let it sink in slightly but not too far. The almond should stick up out of the chocolate for an interesting look. Return to freezer until hard, about 10 minutes.

Remove the Almond Joys from their mold by pressing on the back side of the mold, releasing the contents into your hand.

*How to store:* Store in a covered glass container in the refrigerator with wax paper between the layers for up to a month, or in the freezer for up to 3 months.

---

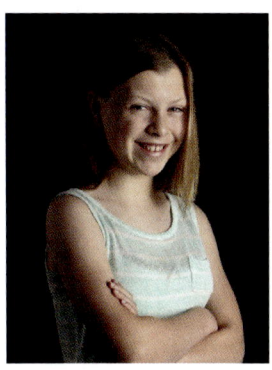

# Snickerdoodles

*Makes about 4 dozen*

**Hanna's Favorite Family Recipe**
*Adapted from the "Betty Crocker Cooky Book."*

These classic cinnamony cookies are a staple in Hanna's house.

*Dough*

1 ½ cups granulated sugar

½ cup unsalted butter, at room temperature

½ cup shortening, at room temperature

2 eggs

2 ¾ cups flour

2 tsp cream of tartar

1 tsp baking soda

½ tsp salt

*Topping*

¼ cup granulated sugar

2 tsp cinnamon

Preheat oven to 400 degrees F.

In the bowl of a stand mixer (or use a hand-held mixer) beat the sugar, butter and shortening until light and fluffy. Add the eggs, one at a time, mixing until well incorporated. Stir in flour, cream of tartar, baking soda and salt.

In a small bowl, mix the ¼ cup sugar and the cinnamon. Shape the dough into 1 1/4-inch balls. Roll balls in the cinnamon-sugar mixture. Place 2 inches apart on ungreased cookie sheet. Bake for 8-10 minutes, or until set. Use a spatula to transfer to wire racks and allow to cool.

# Skillet Blackberry-Blueberry Cobbler

Serves 8-10

**Emma's Favorite Family Recipe**

Every summer Emma's extended family heads to their lake cabin in northwestern Washington State, where they pick blackberries along the country roads and blueberries from the giant bush her great-great grandfather planted beside the lake. Then her mom turns the berries into a biscuit-topped cobbler served warm with vanilla ice cream on the side. It's a family tradition everyone looks forward to, especially Emma. Even better, the biscuits are easy to make and just as good on their own as a morning or afternoon treat spread with honey or jam.

*Biscuits*

3 cups all-purpose flour

1 Tbsp baking powder

1 tsp salt

1 Tbsp sugar, plus more for sprinkling

1 stick (4 oz) cold unsalted butter, cut into 1/4-inch cubes

1 1/4 cups heavy cream, half and half or milk

Melted butter, for brushing

*Filling*

6 cups blackberries

3 cups blueberries

1/2 cup granulated sugar

3 Tbsp cornstarch

*To make the biscuits:* In a large bowl, whisk together the flour, baking powder, salt and sugar. Add the butter and cut it in with a pastry cutter until the mixture looks a bit like cornmeal scattered with some larger pieces of butter. (Alternatively you can do this in a food processor.)

Make a well in the center of the flour and pour in the cream or milk. Fold the dry ingredients into the wet until incorporated into a shaggy dough. Turn out onto a lightly floured surface and briefly knead into a cohesive mass.

Pat the dough out into a large rectangle. Fold the sides of the dough over on itself like you're folding a letter, then fold in half. Pat it out again and repeat. (This helps create flaky layers.) Pat the dough into a 3/4-inch to 1-inch thick circle and cut into rounds using a 2 1/2-inch biscuit cutter. Gently push the scraps together and cut out as many more as you can (you should get about 8 or 9).

Arrange the biscuits on a parchment-lined baking sheet, cover with plastic wrap or a towel, and freeze for 15 minutes while you preheat the oven to 375 degrees F.

*Recipe continued on next page >*

**Skillet Blackberry-Blueberry Cobbler** *continued...*

*To make the filling:* In a large bowl combine the blackberries, blueberries, sugar and cornstarch. Pour into a large cast iron skillet or baking dish and bake fruit in the preheated oven for 20 minutes or until bubbling. Remove from oven, increase heat to 425 degrees F. Arrange frozen biscuits on top of the hot fruit, brush the tops with melted butter, sprinkle with sugar, and bake another 20 minutes or until biscuits are golden brown and cooked through.

Serve warm, with vanilla ice cream of course.

*Note:* You can freeze the biscuits on the baking sheet until hard, then pack into ziptop bags to bake whenever the craving strikes. If baking the biscuits on their own, preheat the oven to 425 degrees F. Arrange frozen biscuits in a buttered baking dish or cast iron skillet just big enough to hold them side by side. They should just barely touch, which will help them support each other as they rise. Brush the tops with melted butter and bake for 15 to 20 minutes, until golden brown.

# Chocolate Bliss Macaroons

*Makes about 2 dozen*

**Jia Patton**
*From the cookbook "Celebrate Life!"*

*Jia Patton was the head of her own cooking school for over fourteen years. She taught the importance of using organic and local fruits and vegetables and she showed others how they could add nutrition to their diets. She is the recipe author for John Robbins's May All Be Fed, Diet for a New World.*

This dish is the perfect dessert, sweet food gift, or energy-packed treat to pull together at the last moment. The chocolatey cocoa along with the crumbly and crispy coconut make these macaroons addictive. If you don't have a silicone candy mold, you can just form the mixture into balls and set on a parchment-lined baking sheet.

2 cups unsweetened shredded coconut

1 cup cacao powder or cocoa powder

2 tsp cinnamon

1 pinch sea salt or other good sea salt

½ cup coconut oil, melted

½ cup honey or other liquid sweetener

In a large mixing bowl, stir together the coconut, cacao (or cocoa) powder, cinnamon and salt. In a small liquid measuring cup, combine the coconut oil and honey. Pour the liquid ingredients over the dry and stir well until evenly coated.

Using a silicon candy mold, fill each cavity with the batter, pressing it in firmly and making it level with the top of the mold. Put into the freezer to harden, about 15 minutes, or in the refrigerator, about 30 minutes. Remove the Chocolate Bliss from the molds by pressing on the back side of the mold, releasing their contents into your hand.

*How to Store:* Store in a covered glass container in the refrigerator with wax paper between the layers for up to a month, or freeze for up to 3 months.